PROSPECTS
for the NINETIES

ALL ENGLAND

Trends and Tables from the English Church Census, with Denominations and Churchmanships

**Compiled and Edited by
Peter Brierley**

This is one of eleven volumes making up the English Church Census results

All royalties from this book have been put towards
the cost of ongoing research on the Church

MARC Europe
London
1991

British Library Cataloguing in Publication Data
Prospects for the Nineties: trends and tables from the
   English church census.
   1. England. Churches. Attendance
   I. Brierley, Peter *1938*- II. MARC Europe
   306.6

   ISBN 1-85321-112-5

First published in Great Britain 1991

Published by MARC Europe
Vision Building, 4 Footscray Road
Eltham, London SE9 2TZ

MARC Europe is a registered charity

Photoset and printed in Great Britain
by Stanley L Hunt (Printers) Ltd
Midland Road, Rushden, Northants NN10 9UA

CONTENTS

Page

FOREWORD

Sir John Boreham
Former Head of the Government Statistical Service

Condorcet, the eighteenth century French philosopher, believed that laws should not be judged by the intentions of legislators nor religions by texts, but by their real effects, as social institutions modified by the practices and beliefs of the people. It is taking quite a time, but we are moving towards his conception of an informed democracy.

On the ancient foundations of broad but shallow demographic and census information we have, in the last hundred years, added, successively, more probing sample surveys of family expenditure, general household characteristics, travel, readership, criminal activities, voting intentions, social attitudes and what-have-you. It is now possible to compile the annual book, *Social Trends,* which would have pleased Condorcet by offering a portrait of contemporary British life.

We are still, however, miles or decades away from being an informed democracy. Not enough statisticians talk or write in a way that makes listening or reading a pleasure, not a duty. And since more than half the people left school before they were 16 years old it is the spiced and over-dramatised mass media that get read, not *Social Trends,* still less the *Journal of the Royal Statistical Society.*

However, measurement goes on and the English Church Census of 1989 falls in to the onward march of Condorcet's survey soldiers. (Could we have a social scientists' anthem, words by Hughes, music by Williamson?)

The Christian churches have declined in membership and influence. It is easy but wrong to think that they don't matter any more. Of course, we all say, Christian ethics are deeply diffused through all our beliefs. Five out of every six adults say that they believe that extra-marital sex is wrong. Two out of every three say that they believe that fiddling expenses or pocketing too much change is wrong.

It's not so easy to know how widely those claimed beliefs are bodied forth in action. Present rates suggest that divorce will be the end of one marriage in every three and in about a third of divorces adultery is the named ground. There is one adult per 200 adult population found guilty or cautioned for burglary, robbery, theft or handling stolen goods.

However actions and beliefs are related, the English Church Census of 1989 shows that 10 per cent of adults went to church on that Sunday in October 1989. The Christian churches are unquestionably a major social institution. Together with the practices and beliefs of the people they continue to affect the lives of all the population.

This volume of statistics from the English Church Census is a source that social statisticians cannot ignore. Roll on the day when *all* the members of an informed British democracy will know and understand the figures.

FOREWORD

Most Rev Dr George Carey
Archbishop of Canterbury

Without any question the survey undertaken by MARC Europe is the most thorough and comprehensive ever done of English churchgoing. It is therefore a significant sociological "map" of the Christian presence which still continues to make an important contribution to the life of our nation.

The importance of this analysis for the Christian churches is self-evident. We are talking of this decade as a decade of evangelism and the research study reveals the reality of the task facing the many Christian Churches. First it gives us a picture of the challenge facing us. Even though such an analysis does not and cannot give us statistics concerning quality of Church life or good work done in the name of the Church, it does show that decline in attendance continues. One area I looked at first of all, was our ministry among young people and we see that we are not holding our youngsters in the faith. This and other data constitute serious and uncomfortable realities for us all.

Second, the challenge is there to be met and addressed. Far from presenting with hopeless conclusions, the study presents us with interesting data concerning sections of the church where growth has taken place and there are possibly clues here for other bodies to consider. It may well be the case, for example, that this survey will act as a stimulus to our growing ecumenical convergence as we share insights into those factors that make for growth and decline.

I am personally clear that MARC Europe has given us in this volume a most important tool to guide our thinking and confound our complacency. It will provide not only the catalyst for the urgent task of sharing faith today, but I believe that it gives us crucial data for strategic planning as we seek to find ways of meeting the spiritual needs of our fellow countrymen and women and to show the true relevance of worship.

METHODOLOGY, NOTES AND DEFINITIONS

Abbreviations

★   Less than 50 attenders/members

†   Too few churches to justify giving any percentages

( )   Brackets round a number indicate it is based on very small numbers of churches (usually between 10 and 20) and therefore less reliable than other figures

12   Figures in *italics* are percentages

12   Upright figures are actual numbers

⇨   Percentages sum to 100% horizontally

⇩   Percentages sum to 100% vertically

—   There are none in this category

n/a   No information is available

└ ½ ┘   The percentage covers all the columns spanned by the brackets

Introduction

On 15th October 1989 a census of the churches in England was undertaken under the auspices of MARC Europe. It was sponsored by World Vision of Britain, the Evangelical Alliance and MARC Europe. This report, *Prospects for the Nineties,* gives tables emerging from the analysis of the data collected. The book *'Christian' England* provides a commentary on the results as well as highlighting the key results across the country, and also contains a description of the reasons for the study, how it was prepared, its Council of Reference, and why we sought to approach all churches rather than just a sample, which readers may wish to consult.

This census is built on earlier studies conducted in England in 1979, Wales in 1982 and Scotland in 1984. The questionnaire did however contain some questions not included in these earlier studies, notably those asking for the age of the church/congregation, its churchmanship, and the preferred ways of supporting the Third World. The actual questionnaire is reproduced overleaf; the original was printed in two colours. Two pilot studies were undertaken in the twelve months prior to the main mailing, each of 200 churches.

A single Sunday was taken rather than a month of Sundays partly because it simplified the work of completing the form, partly to aid publicity, partly because statistically the accuracy of a single Sunday count would on balance be as accurate as an average over a month, partly because this gave a fuller and quicker response in the pilot testing it, and partly because the month of October 1989 contained five Sundays which would have caused special confusion, since many churches have different service arrangements operating on a fifth Sunday. The date chosen avoided festivals, the main holiday periods, the majority of half-terms, and the first Sunday of the month when many churches have Family or other special services. It was also a day which saw bright, pleasant weather over the whole of England. It was as "normal" a Sunday as might be expected. Some churches indicated even so that the Sunday chosen was not typical for them. Some had a Christening service and/or "mourning party" that Sunday afternoon which increased their numbers uncharacteristically. Some churches excluded such numbers, but others included them. In the absence of other information we used the data as given. A few churches took the count the Sunday before or after knowing that October 15th would be unusual.

The response

There were an estimated 38,607 churches at the time of the Census, and usable replies were received from 69.7%. The actual rate varied from county to county, and denomination to denomination, and the individual response rates are shown at the top of the first page for each county or denomination.

About 45% responded initially, and a further 12% after a reminder was sent out. This first reminder was not sent to Roman Catholic churches as their normal annual day for counting mass attendance fell on 29th October, two weeks after Census Sunday, and we suggested that one count be used for both purposes to ease the administrative load, which many priests followed. A second reminder, and a first to Roman Catholic churches, was sent out at the beginning of December, and drew another 10%. A final reminder to the Catholic churches in January, and an extraction of relevant details of 500 Anglican churches from records held at Church House, for whose help and co-operation we are most grateful, made the final response as given. Many Afro-Caribbean churches were telephoned for relevant information, a large task willingly undertaken by the Census Administrator, Dr Kemi Ajayi, and her helpers.

It is now known that not every church was in fact included. This is largely due to the difficulty of locating new independent churches which are currently starting quite quickly. The number omitted is estimated at about 800 churches, with a probable additional church attendance in the Independent sector of 40,000 adults. The tables in this volume exclude these figures.

Who was included?

The Census was intended to cover all Christian denominations, including all Free, Protestant, Anglican, Catholic and Orthodox churches, that is, all those accepting the Trinitarian formula of belief in God the Father, God the Son, and God the Holy Spirit in one Essence. This excluded Jehovah's Witnesses, Mormons, Christian Scientists, Christadelphians, Swedenborgians, Jews, Muslims, Hindus and other non-Trinitarian or non-Christian groups.

We separately identified and counted churches with two or more places of worship in distinct communities, such as linked Church of England parishes where the parish churches were still in use. In team ministries each congregation counted as a unit, unless they all met unitedly together, when they were treated as a single congregation.

The basic unit

The basic unit of the Census was early established as a

ENGLISH CHURCH CENSUS

YOUR NAME AND ADDRESS: Please amend if necessary

BASIC INFORMATION

1. Name of Church/Fellowship ....

2. Postal Address of church premises ....

....

.... Postcode .... Telephone No ....

3. Name of Minister/Leader ....

4. Is the person named in question 3 responsible for other congregations as well?

Yes ☐   No ☐

If yes, how many? ☐   A form should have been received for each church for which this person is responsible. If not, please write below the details of other churches or attach a list so that we can check our records.

Name ....

Town/Village ....

MEMBERS

5. Please indicate the number of <u>members</u> belonging to your Church/Congregation on each of these dates:

15 October 1989	mid-October 1985
☐	☐

ATTENDANCE

6. Please indicate the total attendance <u>at this church</u> on 15 October 1989. (If there was no service on this date, please see note below)*. Please also indicate the total attendance for an average Sunday in October 1985, that is, four years ago. Where more than one morning service is held, please add the total attendances at each service together.

	15 October 1989	Average Sunday in October 1985
Total number of adults (aged 15 and above) attending at <u>all</u> morning services	☐	☐
Total number of adults attending at <u>all</u> afternoon or evening services	☐	☐
Estimated number of adults attending more than one service	☐	☐
Total number of children present in services **BUT NOT** attending Sunday School, Bible Class, etc	☐	☐
Total number of children (aged 14 and under) attending Sunday School, Bible Class, etc	☐	☐

* <u>If there was no service in this church on 15 October 1989,</u> please give instead the figures for the most recent Sunday on which the congregation met for worship and insert here the date of the Sunday for which you are providing figures:

Date of last service ☐

NOW PLEASE TURN OVER

AGE & SEX

7. We appreciate that it is difficult, but it would be a great help if you could please estimate the approximate numbers, by sex and age group, of those attending this church, on Sunday, 15 October 1989 (or, if your church had no service on that day, the previous Sunday on which services were held).

	MALE	FEMALE
Children aged 14 and under		
Teenagers aged 15-19		
Young adults 20-29		
Adults 30-44		
Adults 45-64		
Older people aged 65 and over		

CHURCHMANSHIP

8. Which of these terms, or which combination of them, would best describe your congregation? **Please tick no more than three.**

Anglo-Catholic ☐		Charismatic ☐	
Liberal ☐		Low Church ☐	
Catholic ☐		Orthodox ☐	
Evangelical ☐		Radical ☐	
Broad ☐		Other ☐	please specify ....

SETTING

9. Please indicate which of these terms would best describe the community in which the majority of your congregation live. **Please tick only one box.**

City Centre ☐		Separate Town ☐	
Inner City ☐		Other Built-up area ☐	
Council Estate ☐		Rural: Commuter/dormitory area ☐	
Suburban/Urban fringe ☐		Rural: Other areas ☐	

10. In what year was your church/congregation founded? ☐

MISCELLANEOUS

11. Which of the following types of Third World Community Aid do you think your church would most wish to support? Please tick those one or two items which would most closely represent your congregation's preferences.

☐ Types of activity, such as water supply, irrigation, medical projects, etc.
☐ Specific geographical areas, such as particular countries or districts in which you take a special interest.
☐ Aid to named communities, such as particular villages or tribal groups.
☐ Aid to named individuals, such as sponsored children.
☐ Aid to be administered through local churches overseas.
☐ Evangelism and other missionary work.
☐ Other (Please specify) ....
☐ We prefer not to give support to this type of work.

Name of respondent (in capitals) ....

Telephone Number .... Date ....

Thank you very much for your help. Please return the form to MARC Europe, FREEPOST, Cosmos House, 6 Homesdale Road, Bromley, Kent BR2 9UW. Telephone 01-460 3999

congregation, which was defined as "a body of people meeting on a Sunday in the same premises primarily for public worship at regular intervals". The key elements of this definition are:

"a body of people", that is, a congregation is the basic unit rather than a church. This means that where a church building is used by more than one group, each separate group counted as a unit. This covers the situation in some rural areas where an Anglican Parish Church may also be used for the celebration of Roman Catholic mass. On the other hand, where a church had united into one congregation, the fact that it is recognised by both the Methodists and United Reformed Church (URC), for example, does not mean that it counted as two congregations, unless separate services, with essentially different groups of people, were held.

"on a Sunday" meant that those groups meeting for prayer and/or Bible Study mid-week, and services at crematoria, were excluded. But a modification from Sunday to Saturday was allowed for the Seventh Day Adventists and Saturday evening Catholic services.

"primarily for public worship". Public worship was taken to mean where ordinary members of the public would be able to attend, if necessary with notice. Thus religious communities holding services not open to the public, or closed groups like prisons, were not included. Schools, colleges, university chaplaincies, military bases, religious orders and others that advertise service times were taken to be open to the public, and therefore included. Prisons, hospitals and services in old folks' homes were generally excluded on these grounds. A few hospitals whose services were known to be open to the passing public were included. It was not particularly difficult to identify religious services in schools, colleges and universities, but hospital services tend to rotate around denominations, making it difficult to track down the person responsible. Prison services are not always open to the public, and services in residential care facilities proved almost impossible to identify comprehensively. Many of the people in these groups might still be on the registers of their local churches, creating a situation where some might be counted twice, so excluding them erred on the side of caution.

"at regular intervals" allowed for the situation, common in rural areas, where services are not held every week. If a service was held at least monthly numbers were included; those held less regularly were not. This also eliminated special events such as Christian holiday gatherings, conferences, conventions and private chapels used for occasional services such as funerals or festivals.

"in the same premises". This was introduced to identify a congregation specifically by its geographical location. Where a group of people have been known to rotate around people's houses Sunday by Sunday they have generally not been included.

The above definition meant that a few worshippers were excluded from the Census count. The numbers we do have however relate to public worshippers coming to church or chapel in the normally understood sense of what it means to "go to church".

Details collected

Church membership was collected for 1985 and 1989. The definition of membership is generally that used by the denomination in question, and this varies from one denomination to another. The Roman Catholic Church estimates of their population include children. Some Anglican churches gave two figures, one for their parish and one for their Electoral Roll. The latter was used.

The 1975 and 1979 attendance and membership figures were rounded to the nearest thousand for publication. Where necessary the figures have been restored to the nearest hundred in this volume. If a change to the previously published figures occurs when rounded to the nearest thousand this is indicated in a footnote.

Church attendance was collected for 1985 and 1989. Sunday School attendance and children attending service but not in Sunday School, Bible Class, etc, were requested separately, as was the number of individual adults who attended *both* morning and evening (where two services were held). This latter figure of "twicers" was not always given. Where churches holding two services did not state a figure, it was assumed that the proportion would be the same as for those churches which did give details, for that county and denomination. Afternoon services were counted as evening services for the purposes of this study.

Where the Report gives figures of church *attenders* this refers to individuals attending at least one service morning or evening, that is, "twicers" are counted only once. In the "Size of church by weekly attendance" tables those going twice are counted twice.

Some churches were unable to give a 1985 attendance figure; it was assumed that the 1985 attendance would be as for other churches (who gave both figures) in that county for that denomination. Churches which held no service on 15th October 1989 were requested instead to give details of their most recent service and its date. If the date was up to four weeks previous the data were used, but not if the last service was earlier than this (for example, Easter 1989).

Child attendance. Not every church has a Sunday School, and not every child going to church attends a Sunday School even if there is one. Details of the latter were obtained by comparing the number of children under 15 attending the church and the number going to Sunday School. Sometimes the numbers of young people associated with a church bore little resemblance to adult membership. Child attendance is the *total* of those present in services and not attending Sunday School, and of those attending Sunday School. The percentage in the latter category is given for 1985 and 1989.

Age and sex of attenders. These were collected for 1989 congregations only, and were generally estimated by the person completing the questionnaire. This question was not always answered, but the degree of response, both by denomination and county, is indicated in this Report, expressed as a percentage of all churches in England. Overall 68% of the churches were able to give this information.

A few churches gave figures for age-groups different from those used on the form, or for the age-groups given but not broken down by sex. Estimates based on the civil population in the relevant county were made for these.

Churchmanship. See separate section below on this question.

Environment. Collected for 1989 only, but unlikely to have changed since 1985 in most cases. Eight categories were used, without any fuller explanation other than the description implicit in the category: City Centre, Inner City, Council Estate, Suburban/Urban Fringe, Separate Town, Other Built-up area, Rural: Commuter/Dormitory area, and Rural: Other areas. The question related to the domicile of the majority of the congregation rather than the venue of worship.

Where more than one box was ticked, the specific was preferred over the general. Thus Suburban/Urban Fringe was taken instead of Other Built-up area, Inner City to City Centre, and Council Estate to Other Built-up area.

Age of church/congregation. The date the congregation started to meet rather than the age of the building per se, the difference being especially important for those who have taken over redundant churches, or who hire school halls, etc to meet in.

Where two dates were given, the earlier date was preferred. Where events were supplied rather than dates, the corresponding dates used in the analysis are given below:

Roman Britain	200	Magna Carta	1215
Dark Ages	450	Gothic	1300
Anglo-Saxon	850	Tudor	1500
Norman Conquest	1066	Renaissance	1550
Domesday Book	1087	Stuart	1650
Medieval/MiddleAges/		Regency/Georgian	1720
Norman	1100	Victorian	1875

Third World Community Aid. Asked for 1989 only. Respondents were invited to tick up to two boxes, but as many ticked three, three were used for analysis. Again no description was given in addition to the words used in the actual question, but many gave additional information, often the names of the society(ies) they supported. The first category "types of activity" has been changed to "project activities" in this Report for clarity with other types of support.

Where descriptions of aid to the Third World and charities were specified in the "Other, please specify" box, they were allocated to the questionnaire categories as follows:

Types of activity: Development work, Christian Aid, CAFOD, CWM, Save the Children Fund, Help the Aged, Leprosy Mission, Oxfam, On-going relief and development work.

Specific geographical areas: Immediate Relief, Disasters, Emergencies.

Named communities: Traidcraft.

Named individuals: Sponsored Missionaries.

Administered through local churches: Named church, Tear Fund.

Evangelism/Missionary work: Home missions, Baptist Missionary Society, USPG, CMS, Methodist Overseas Mission, Bible Society, SAMS, Evangelism.

The emphasis was on identifying terms that were similar to the options provided within the questions.

Boxes were sometimes ticked more than three times. Up to three were taken, and these are reflected in this Report exactly as ticked, with the corresponding percentages adding up to over 100% in each table — usually about 185%.

For those concerned with knowing how those ticking more than three boxes were coded, the details follow, using A = Project activities, B = Geographical areas, C = Named Communities, D = Named individuals, E = Administered through local churches, F = Evangelism/missionary work. 68 ticked ABEF and were coded AEF, 39 ABCDEF(DEF), 33 ABDF(ADF), 25 ACEF(CEF), 25 ADEF(DEF), 24 ABCEF(CEF), 19 ABCD(BCD), 17 ABCE(ACE), 14 ABCDE(CDE), 12 BDEF(DEF), 11 ACDE(CDE), 10 ACDF(CDF), 10 BCEF(CEF), 9 ABDEF(DEF), 8 ABCDF(CDF), 8 ABDE(ADE), 6 BCDF(BCD), 5 CDEF(DEF), 4 ACDEF(DEF), 2 BCDE(CDE), 1 ABCE(ACE), 1 BCDEF(DEF).

Civil population. The adult and child figures by county have been taken from the figures published by the Office of Population Censuses and Surveys (OPCS) in their 1984 and 1988 reports *Key population and vital statistics* (Series VS PP1), with the split between 15-19 and 20-29, which this publication does not give, being taken from more detailed figures OPCS publishes.

Isle of Man population. These figures are estimates based on their 1986 census. The rate of change used is that quoted in the 1986 census report and is based on the total adult and child resident population between 1981 and 1986.

Channel Islands population. Estimates of the population of Guernsey and Jersey are from their 1986 censuses. Figures for Sark and Alderney were estimated using 1984 census figures.

Coding

The **Census code** used was a three position identifier, with two digits to represent the county and a third alphabetical character identifying the local government district. In every case, the county and district code which were given were those that pertain to *the location where the congregation meet,* and *not* the address to which the form was sent. In many cases, of course, the two locations would attract the same Census code.

The location of each congregation included in the Census — all 38,600 of them — was checked and coded according to its county and local government district. For the Church of England, this has generally meant checking the location of churches on Ordnance Survey Landranger 1:50,000 maps, which show local government boundaries and churches in sufficient detail to identify the area quite precisely. For other denominations, it has sometimes been sufficient to use much less detailed maps. In the cases of conurbations, which frequently straddle district boundaries, local street maps have been used where possible to locate the churches as precisely as could be done. Nevertheless some judgements have had to be made where information on the location of the church was insufficiently precise to locate it absolutely. A good example of this is the Seven Sisters Road in London, which passes through four local government districts in the space of a few hundred yards; where the street number of the church location is not given, it is impossible to know which district the church actually met in!

Each congregation was given a **denomination code.** The general practice was to use the first position of the denomination code – as a number from 0 to 9 – to identify a broad denominational grouping (Anglican, Baptist, Independent etc), whilst the second position – an alphabetical one – has been used to identify the specific denomination within these broad theological groups.

Each congregation was also assigned an **acquisition code,** which identified the source from which its address was gathered. In the case of Anglican churches, this has almost exclusively been the diocesan directory. The corollary of this is that it would be possible, using the acquisition code as an identifier, to extract from the Census data the returns for churches within a particular diocese – diocesan boundaries are generally not contiguous with county or other local government boundaries. Similar considerations apply to other major denominations publishing directories, so that it is possible to identify members of a particular Methodist District, Baptist Association or URC province for instance.

Component Groups within Denominations
The different denominations were grouped into ten categories for ease of analysis. Which denominations were included in which group are given below.

Methodist
Methodist Church of Great Britain
The Free Methodist Church in the UK
Independent Methodist Church
Wesleyan Reform Union
Other Methodist churches

Baptist
Baptist Union of Great Britain
Gospel Standard Strict Baptist Societies
Grace Baptist Church
Jesus Fellowship Church (Baptist)
Old Baptist Union
Other Baptist Churches

URC
Presbyterian Church in England
The United Reformed Church in England

Independent
Brethren (Open)
Plymouth Brethren No 4
Congregational Federation
Evangelical Fellowship of Congregational Churches
Union of Evangelical Churches
Fellowship of Independent Evangelical Churches
House Churches
Other Non-denominational Churches
New Apostolic Church
Fellowship of Churches of Christ
Liberal Catholic Church
Residential Schools/Colleges
Other Independent Churches

Afro-Caribbean
Apostolic Faith Church
Cherubim & Seraphim Church
Church of God of Prophecy
New Testament Church Assembly
New Testament Church of God
Ransom Church of God Universal Fellowship
Wesleyan Holiness Church
Other Afro-Caribbean churches; 164 separate groups were identified

Pentecostal/Holiness
Apostolic Church
Assemblies of God in UK
Elim Pentecostal Churches
Emmanuel Holiness Church
Church of the Nazarene International
Other Pentecostal Churches

Other Free Churches
Chinese Churches
The Countess of Huntingdon's Connexion
Lutheran Church
Moravian Church in Great Britain
Religious Society of Friends
The Salvation Army
Seventh-day Adventist
Churches for Overseas Nationals
Mission Centres of City Missions and the Shaftesbury Society
Other Churches

Anglican
Church of England
The Free Church of England
The Protestant Evangelical Church of England

Roman Catholic
Roman Catholic Church of England & Wales
Old Roman Catholic Church
Tridentine Institute of our Lady of Walsingham
Croatian Roman Catholic Church
German Roman Catholic Church
Hungarian Roman Catholic Church
Latvian Roman Catholic Church
Lithuanian Roman Catholic Church
Slovene Catholic Mission
Ukrainian Catholic Church
Polish Catholic Church
Other Roman Catholic Churches

Orthodox
Ancient Orthodox Church
Antiochian (Syrian) Orthodox Church
The Orthodox Church of the British Isles
Bulgarian Orthodox Church
Byelorussian Autocephalic Orthodox Church
Greek Orthodox Archdiocese of Thyateira
Romanian Orthodox Church in London
Russian Orthodox Church – Patriarchal Diocese in the UK
Russian Orthodox Church outside Russia
Serbian Orthodox Church
Ukrainian Autocephalous Orthodox Church
Other Orthodox Churches

Analysis

The data collected from the forms was computerised. The totals for each component were grossed up according to the response rate for each denomination and county. The membership totals were then compared with the published denominational totals, and found on average to be 1% higher in 1989 reflecting a tendency for the forms to be returned by the larger churches. The grossed figures were therefore reduced by the appropriate denominational percentage, which was also applied to the number of attenders, so that the ratio of attenders to members remained the same. These denominational percentage reductions averaged 1.2% for the Free Churches, 1.8% for the Roman Catholics, and 24% for the Anglicans, where a number of particularly small rural churches failed to respond. A few other adjustments were made to the data, usually when only partial details were given in certain denominational/county groupings which had just a small number of churches; the direction of trend was however always maintained. The very small response of the Orthodox Churches necessitated special treatment. A comparison of actual and Census attendance figures is given in Table 1 of 'Christian' England. All figures have been rounded to the nearest 100.

The size of English churches was counted on a finer grid than is given in this Report — in groups of five up to 25, then in 25's up to 150, 50's up to 400, and so on. These more detailed percentages may be obtained from MARC Europe. In working out these bands a representative number for each group has been used. This has not been the mid-point as is customary, but, because intermediate groups showed concentrations towards the beginning of each group, a figure of about 10% over the minimum was used instead. Thus the representative numbers used were respectively 1, 12, 30, 55, 110, 165, 220, 330, 440, and 550 (when an over 500 group was included).

Growing churches were defined as those whose attendance had increased by at least 20% over the four years 1985-1989 for churches with 1989 attenders numbering 50 or more, or an increase of at least 100% for churches with fewer than 50 attenders in 1989. These criteria are fairly rigorous, partly to conform with the English, Welsh and Scottish church growth data already published, and partly to ensure that any growth thus recorded was real. Thus a church with 10 attenders in 1985 which grew to 12 in 1989 (a 20% increase) would not be counted as a growing church; but if its 1989 number was 20 or more (a 100% increase) it would have been. A church with 60 attenders in 1985 would be counted as a growing church if its numbers in 1989 were 72 or more (a 20% increase).

Declining churches are defined similarly, but in negative rather than positive terms. Static churches are those which are neither growing nor declining.

The church environment and churchmanship tables give also the percentage of the number of churches, in addition to those of child attenders, adult attenders, and members, in each category, which usually are most interesting to compare. To help the reader more easily understand, arrows have been used to indicate the direction in which the percentages have been taken.

Thus a horizontal arrow (⇨) indicates that the percentages sum to 100% horizontally; the number on which the percentages are based is given in the final column. A vertical arrow (⇩) indicates that the percentages sum to 100% vertically, although the number on which these percentages are based is not usually given since they can be easily derived from the horizontal percentage figures. The same convention of arrow signs has been used in other tables.

Rates of change for attenders and members have been calculated over the four year period based on 1989, and between 1975 and 1979 based on 1979, and 1979 and 1985 based on 1985 to give an historical perspective whenever possible.

Greater London. In the 1979 Census, Inner London was taken as the boundary of the then Inner London Education Authority. For consistency in analysis the same boundaries were used for the 1989 Census, but in order to facilitate a greater understanding of the trends throughout Greater London, both Inner London and Outer London were broken down into four groups of boroughs — North West, North East, South East and South West. The actual boroughs included within each grouping are shown on the map of London on Pages **18** and **291**, but for convenience are listed below:

Inner London North East:
  City of London, Hackney, Islington and Tower Hamlets
Inner London North West:
  Camden, City of Westminster, Hammersmith and Fulham, and Kensington and Chelsea
Inner London South West:
  Lambeth and Wandsworth
Inner London South East:
  Greenwich, Lewisham and Southwark
Outer London North East:
  Barking and Dagenham, Enfield, Haringey, Havering, Newham, Redbridge and Waltham Forest
Outer London North West:
  Barnet, Brent, Ealing, Harrow, Hillingdon and Hounslow
Outer London South West:
  Kingston-upon-Thames, Merton, Richmond-upon-Thames and Sutton
Outer London South East:
  Bexley, Bromley and Croydon

Inner London as officially defined includes Haringey and Newham, here included with Outer London North East, and excludes Greenwich, here included with Inner London South East.

Churchmanship

Respondents were invited to tick up to three boxes in a list of nine categories, and were able to use an "other, please specify" category as well. The nine categories used were based on the results of the pilot studies. The information was completed by the minister, or other person completing the form, to describe his/her congregation not their own personal position.

Not all answered the question adequately. Those who indicated names of denominations, like Church of England or Baptist alone, were not acceptable, and therefore treated as a null response. Those who entered other terms which were not listed were reclassified as follows:

Pentecostal	was classified as Charismatic
Bible based	was classified as Evangelical
Calvinist	was classified as Evangelical
Salvation Army	was classified as Evangelical
Middle of the Road	was classified as Broad
Mixed	was classified as Broad
Average	was classified as Broad

When two boxes were ticked in addition to the "Other" box, the latter was ignored unless it included any of the above. A major principle was to look for words and expressions in the "Other" box that matched those in the choice of boxes presented. "Ecumenical" did not qualify here although it has been useful in identification and collation of ecumenical churches.

The actual number of ticks given for each category on forms with at least one tick, broke down as follows, with the letter used as a code for that category shown:

Table 1: Churchmanship answers

	Term	Number of ticks		Number of ticks	Number of forms
D	Evangelical	9,597	Single designation		12,025
E	Broad	9,074	Double designation		7,274
C	Catholic	4,602	Triple designation		3,630
G	Low Church	3,903	Four or more		50
B	Liberal	3,605			
F	Charismatic	2,872	Total		23,747
A	Anglo-Catholic	1,732			
H	Orthodox	1,639			
I	Radical	574			
J	Other (by itself)	131			
	Total	37,729			

The actual combinations of codes that were used for each category in the analysis in this Report (using the letters indicated) were as follows (any combination not shown was zero):

Catholic (3,439)
C(2,359), CD(118), CDE(138), CDG(11), CDH(14), CDI(12), CDJ(3), CE(487), CEF(20), CEG(19), CEH(67), CEI(12), CEJ(5), CF(26), CFH(5), CFI(2), CH(113), CHI(3), CI(17), CJ(8).

Anglo-Catholic (1,345)
A(751), AC(71), ACD(9), ACE(40), ACF(3), ACG(5), ACH(26), ACI(2), AD(30), ADG(8), ADH(6), ADI(1), AE(207), AEF(14), AEG(31), AEH(23), AEI(3), AEJ(1), AF(29), AFH(1), AFI(2), AG(24), AGH(2), AH(50), AI(5), AJ(1).

Liberal (3,346)
AB(142), ABC(28), ABD(24), ABE(95), ABF(8), ABG(4), ABH(8), ABI(9), ABJ(2), B(482), BC(465), BCD(72), BCE(295), BCF(13), BCG(13), BCH(21), BCI(24), BCJ(3), BD(293), BDG(71), BDH(14), BDI(11), BDJ(5), BE(665), BEF(14), BEG(151), BEH(83), BEI(61), BEJ(3), BF(21), BFG(5), BFH(2), BFI(3), BG(114), BGH(6), BGI(9), BH(37), BHJ(2), BI(56), BIJ(4), BJ(8).

Low Church (2,890)
CG(14), CGH(4), DG(842), DGH(48), DGI(7), DGJ(7), EG(700), EGH(57), EGI(3), EGJ(9), FG(20), FGH(1), FGJ(1), G(1,022), GH(144), GHJ(2), GI(1), GJ(8).

Broad (4,019)
E(3,615), EF(48), EFG(9), EFH(6), EFI(7), EH(282), EHI(1), EHJ(2), EI(27), EJ(22).

Broad Evangelical (1,674)
ADE(37), BDE(218), DE(1,026), DEG(312), DEH(61), DEI(14), DEJ(6).

Mainstream Evangelical (3,907)
D(3,657), DH(160), DHI(3), DHJ(4), DI(42), DIJ(2), DJ(39).

Charismatic Evangelical (2,585)
ADF(30), BDF(41), CDF(68), DEF(178), DF(1,521), DFG(219), DFH(22), DFI(174), DFJ(19), F(310), FJ(3).

All Other Churchmanships (542)
FH(5), FI(24), H(348), HI(4), HJ(1), I(28), IJ(1), J(131).

Six ministers ticked all nine specific boxes, and were coded AEH, four ticked BCDE and were coded BDE, three ticked BCDF and were coded BCF, two each ticked BDEFG (and were coded BDF), BCDEGHI(BEH), DEGH(DEG), and all the following occurred once each with the classification used shown in brackets: ABCDE(BDE), ABCDEFG(AEF), ABCDEGI(BEG), ABCDF(ABD), ABCDI(ABD), ABCH(ABH), ABCI(ABC), ABDEFG(BDF), ABDF(ABD), ABEG(ABG), ABEGI(ABI), ACDG(ADG), ADEH(ADE), BCDEG(BEG), BCDFH(BCD), BCEFI(BCI), BCEH(BCH), BCEHI(BCI), BDEFG(BDF), BDEFI(BDF), BDEG(BDG), BDEGH(BDG), BDFG(BDF), BDFI(BDF), BEFI(BFI), BEGH(BGH), BEGI(BEI), CDFI(DFI), CDGI(CDI), DEFH(DFH), DFGI(DFI).

Local Ecumenical Projects (LEPs)
It proved much more difficult to distinguish LEPs than we had expected. An LEP is essentially an expression of unity at the local level by various denominational groups. LEPs are organised in various ways and the different churches involved may well have differing perceptions of their association. Nor do the terms used by the churches indicating their level of involvement lend themselves to ready classification, but in working on these Kemi Ajayi suggested the following types:

United congregation. Here services are held which do not distinguish the various denominations making up that congregation. A totally new congregation evolves with no particular emphasis on the doctrine of one church or the other.

Shared building. A number of denominational churches use the same premises for services. If this kind of arrangement is not combined with another it means that all that is common to the denominations involved is the use of the building. Their services would be held at different times and their congregations would be separate.

Shared ministry. Services are held by the various denominations which would be conducted by the different ministers of those denominations. This may not necessarily imply a total union of the denominations at the local congregational level. A pulpit exchange is often all that happens.

Shared congregation. Joint services are held whereby all the various denominational groups represented in the LEP come together for a service. This could be once a week, say at an evening service, or once a month. Frequently though, a shared congregation implies a united congregation.

Local covenant. Agreements reached by the denominations are limited to the churches at the local village or town level. This would need to be confirmed and ratified by the denominational headquarters/authorities for it to be recognised as a LEP. The congregations would meet together periodically for a joint service or a day of prayer as an ecumenical activity.

The Sponsoring Body. Some LEPs function as a committee whereby a dialogue is carried out between the leadership of the churches. Some such committees hold prayer meetings regularly and discuss issues of common concern to their locality. Such committees may

Table 2: Local Ecumenical Projects 1989

						United Congregation	Loose LEP	Mixed Group	Total
Two denominations									
Methodist	URC					259	7	27	293
Methodist		Anglican				179	107	6	292
	URC		Baptist			61	–	5	66
	URC	Anglican				29	13	–	42
		Anglican		Catholic		–	27	1	28
		Anglican	Baptist			8	15	3	26
Methodist			Baptist			10	2	–	12
			Baptist		Other[a]	10	–	–	10
	URC				Other[b]	6	–	–	6
Methodist					Other[a]	4	–	–	4
Methodist					Other[c]	–	1	–	1
Methodist					Other[d]	–	1	–	1
Three denominations									
Methodist	URC	Anglican				56	24	–	80
Methodist		Anglican		Catholic		5	35	–	40
Methodist	URC		Baptist			19	1	3	23
	URC	Anglican		Catholic		–	14	–	23
		Anglican	Baptist	Catholic		–	5	3	8
	URC	Anglican	Baptist			6	–	–	6
Methodist		Anglican	Baptist			–	6	–	6
Methodist		Anglican			Other[d]	–	4	–	4
	URC		Baptist		Other[a]	2	–	–	2
Four denominations									
Methodist	URC	Anglican	Baptist			52	15	–	67
Methodist	URC	Anglican		Catholic		10	28	4	42
Methodist	URC	Anglican			Other[d]	3	7	–	10
		Anglican	Baptist	Catholic	Other[d]	–	7	–	7
Methodist		Anglican	Baptist	Catholic		4	2	–	6
Methodist	URC		Baptist		Other[d]	1	3	–	4
	URC	Anglican	Baptist	Catholic		–	2	–	2
Five denominations									
Methodist	URC	Anglican	Baptist	Catholic		14	15	–	29
Methodist	URC	Anglican	Baptist		Other[d]	–	–	3	3
Six denominations									
Methodist	URC	Anglican	Baptist	Catholic	Other[d]	–	4	–	4
			Total			738	345	55	1,138

[a]Congregational   [b]Moravian   [c]Assemblies of God   [d]Unspecified

be the spring board for joint activities by the churches involved, for instance, as ecumenical groups meeting during Lent. Some have also initiated community projects or provided drop-in centres in their localities.

Mixed group. It is quite possible to find two different denominations coming together as a united church, and yet combining with one or two other denominations as an LEP either in a shared building or pulpit exchange. Various combinations of the above types can also occur, depending on the kinds of arrangements that operated at a local level. Table 2 on the previous page lists the various combinations that are known to occur. It should be noted that these projects are based at the local, congregational, level rather than at the wider denominational, or territorial, level. The denominational headquarters are, of course, aware of these LEPs and some indicate the churches belonging to them in their handbooks.

Of these 1,138 LEPs, 65% or nearly two-thirds are united congregations, 30% are loose LEPs and the remaining 5% are mixed groups. Altogether, 781 or 69% concern two denominations, 183 or 16% three, 138 or 12% four, 32 or 3% five, and 4 or 0% six denominations. The Methodists are involved in 920 or 81%, the Anglicans in 716 or 63%, the URC in 693 or 61%, the Baptists in 281 or 25%, the Roman Catholics in 180 or 16% (they are in few groups of two or three), and Others account for the remaining 59 or 5%. Details of many of these were published in the 1988 *Register of Local Ecumenical Projects and Sponsoring Bodies* by the Consultative Committee for LEPs in England.

For the Census the figures have been split for the LEPs equally between participating bodies; thus if a Methodist/URC reported a congregation of 120 this would be counted as ½ a Methodist Church with 60 people and ½ a URC church with 60 people.

Unfortunately comparative figures on numbers of LEPs in earlier years are not available. The LEPs as a group gave the best response of all to the Census – 83%.

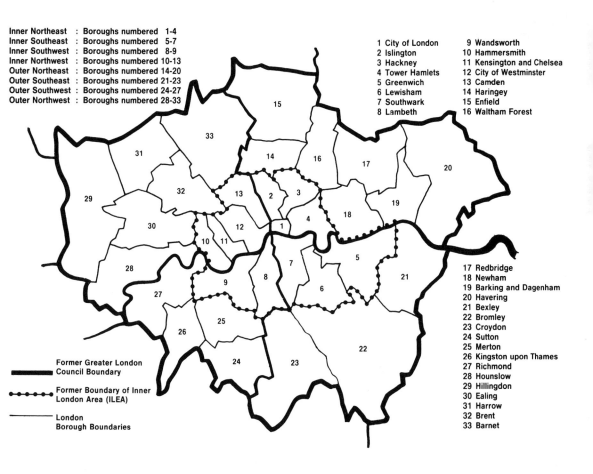

Inner Northeast : Boroughs numbered 1-4
Inner Southeast : Boroughs numbered 5-7
Inner Southwest : Boroughs numbered 8-9
Inner Northwest : Boroughs numbered 10-13
Outer Northeast : Boroughs numbered 14-20
Outer Southeast : Boroughs numbered 21-23
Outer Southwest : Boroughs numbered 24-27
Outer Northwest : Boroughs numbered 28-33

1 City of London
2 Islington
3 Hackney
4 Tower Hamlets
5 Greenwich
6 Lewisham
7 Southwark
8 Lambeth
9 Wandsworth
10 Hammersmith
11 Kensington and Chelsea
12 City of Westminster
13 Camden
14 Haringey
15 Enfield
16 Waltham Forest
17 Redbridge
18 Newham
19 Barking and Dagenham
20 Havering
21 Bexley
22 Bromley
23 Croydon
24 Sutton
25 Merton
26 Kingston upon Thames
27 Richmond
28 Hounslow
29 Hillingdon
30 Ealing
31 Harrow
32 Brent
33 Barnet

Former Greater London Council Boundary

Former Boundary of Inner London Area (ILEA)

London Borough Boundaries

ALL ENGLAND

Total adult population: 38,832,800

Change in last four years: +2%

Total child population: 8,902,500

Change in last four years: −1%

1989 adult church attenders as
percentage of adult population: 10%[7]

1989 child church attenders as
percentage of child population: 14%[8]

Percentage of churches
responding: 70%

Adult and Child Attenders and Membership

Attenders	Metho-dist	Baptist	URC	Inde-pendent	Afro-Carib-bean	Pente-costal	Other	TOTAL Free Churches	Anglican	Roman Catholic	TOTAL Christian[2]
Children											
1975	208,000	92,000	55,000	93,000	39,000	30,000	44,000	561,000	445,000	474,000	1,483,000
⇩ 4 years	−16%	−5%	−7%	0%	+5%	+10%	−2%	−7%	−7%	0%	−5%
1979	174,000	87,000	51,000	93,000	41,000	33,000	43,000	522,000	415,000[1]	476,000	1,416,000
⇩ 6 years	−21%	−10%	−16%	+28%	−7%	+7%	−19%	−7%	−11%	−11%	−10%
1985	**138,100**	**78,200**	**42,700**	**118,600**	**38,200**	**35,400**	**34,900**	**486,100**	**367,300**	**424,700**	**1,280,900**
⇩ 4 years	−16%	−9%	−17%	+12%	−7%	+6%	−12%	−6%	−5%	−3%	−5%
1989	**116,200**	**71,500**	**35,300**	**132,700**	**35,600**	**37,400**	**30,600**	**459,300**	**348,000**	**411,300**	**1,221,500**
At Sunday School 1985 %	93	90	89	81	76	80	87	87	71	—	—
1989 %	**86**	**87**	**81**	**78**	**77**	**78**	**84**	**82**	**64**	**—**	**—**
Adults											
1975	454,000	193,000	150,000	167,000	55,000	78,000	112,000[1]	1,209,000	1,302,000	1,576,000[1]	4,093,000
⇩ 4 years	−2%	+5%	−7%	+23%	+20%	+13%	−12%	+3%	−4%	−4%	−2%
1979	447,000	203,000	139,000	206,000	66,000	88,000	98,000[1]	1,247,000	1,256,000	1,515,000[1]	4,025,000
⇩ 6 years	−6%	−3%	−13%	+25%	+2%	−4%	−17%	−1%	−6%	−12%	−7%
1985	**420,800**	**196,200**	**121,400**	**257,500**	**67,500**	**84,900**	**81,400**	**1,229,700**	**1,181,000**	**1,335,900**	**3,755,000**
⇩ 4 years	−6%	+2%	−6%	+14%	+1%	+11%	+2%	+2%	−3%	−2%	−1%
1989	**396,100**	**199,400**	**114,000**	**292,800**	**68,500**	**95,200**	**83,000**	**1,249,000**	**1,143,900**	**1,304,600**	**3,706,900**
Average adults attending[3] 1979	59	92	76	60	80	93	81	69	74	412	104
1989	**59**	**85**	**68**	**71**	**72**	**95**	**57**	**68**	**70**	**341**	**96**

Membership	Metho-dist	Baptist	URC	Inde-pendent	Afro-Carib-bean	Pente-costal	Other	TOTAL Free Churches	Anglican	Roman Catholic[4]	TOTAL Christian[2]
1975	515,000	167,000[1]	192,000[1]	137,000	47,000	63,000	131,000[1]	1,252,000	1,999,000	3,994,600[1]	7,447,600
⇩ 4 years	−8%	−3%	−14%	+23%	+33%	+6%	+1%	−2%	−5%	+1%	−1%
1979	473,000	162,000	166,000	169,000	62,600[1]	67,000	132,000[1]	1,231,600	1,907,000[1]	4,036,000[1]	7,381,600
⇩ 6 years	−8%	+3%	−23%	+18%	+7%	−10%	−23%	−6%	−12%	−1%	−4%
1985	**435,800**	**166,800**	**127,200**	**198,600**	**65,400**	**60,100**	**101,600**	**1,155,500**	**1,675,300**	**4,006,500**	**7,057,300**
⇩ 4 years	−3%	+2%	−6%	+12%	+4%	+13%	+2%	+2%	−7%	+5%	+1%
1989	**422,200**	**170,600**	**119,900**	**222,100**	**68,200**	**68,000**	**103,200**	**1,174,200**	**1,559,000**	**4,197,100**	**7,162,400**
Members per church 1979	62	73	91	47	101	79	85	67	112	1,099	189
1989	**63**	**73**	**71**	**51**	**105**	**72**	**66**	**64**	**95**	**1,037**	**186**
Number of Churches[6] 1979	7,636[1]	2,211[1]	1,829[1]	3,430	822[1]	950	1,456[1]	18,334	16,960[1]	3,673	39,064
[6] 1989	**6,740**	**2,339**	**1,681**	**4,123[5]**	**949**	**1,002**	**1,462**	**18,296**	**16,373**	**3,824**	**38,607**

[1] Revised figure   [2] This column includes Orthodox Church figures of child attendance of 3,000, 3,000, 2,800 and 2,900; adult attendance
figures of 6,000, 7,000, 8,400 and 9,400; and membership figures of 202,000, 207,000, 220,000 and 232,100 for 1975, 1979, 1985 and
1989 respectively; with 97 congregations in 1979 and 114 in 1989
[3] Sunday morning and evening adult congregations combined (where both held), excluding twicers
[4] Membership figures are Roman Catholic population   [5] Including 308 residential schools/colleges
[6] The 1989 figures count Local Ecumenical Projects proportionately; the 1979 figures count them in full. The 1979 number of Methodist,
URC and Anglican churches, especially, are therefore slightly too high
[7] 11% in 1979   [8] 14% in 1979

Age and sex of churchgoers 1979 and 1989

Age-Group	Population 1979			Churchgoers in 1979			Churchgoers in 1989[1]			Population 1989		
	Men %	Women %	Total %	Men %	Women %	Total %	Men %	Women %	Total %	Men %	Women %	Total %
Under 15	11	10	21	13	13	26	12	13	25	10	9	19
15-19	4	4	8	4	5	9	3	4	7	4	4	8
20-29	7	7	14	5	6	11	4	6	10	8	8	16
30-44	10	9	19	7	9	16	7	10	17	10	10	20
45-64	11	12	23	9	11	20	9	13	22	11	11	22
65 and over	6	9	15	7	11	18	7	12	19	6	9	15
All ages	49	51	100	45	55	100	42	58	100	49	51	100

[1] This table is based on responses from 68% of all churches in England

Church environment

Percentage of all churches 1989 ⇨ %	City Centre 4	Inner City 7	Council Estate 6	Suburban/ Urban Fringe 22	Separate Town 12	Other built-up area 4	Rural area: Commuter dormitory 16	Rural area: Other 29	ALL Churches 100
Children attending:									
1985	49,800	106,500	103,000	461,500	198,400	57,000	170,700	134,000	1,280,900
⇩ 4 years	−7%	0%	−3%	−5%	−5%	+1%	−5%	−8%	−5%
1989	46,300	106,400	99,700	437,000	188,800	57,600	163,000	122,700	1,221,500
Percentage of total ⇨ %	4	9	8	36	15	5	13	10	100
Adults attending:									
1985	211,600	384,300	300,600	1,291,900	580,100	170,400	404,100	412,000	3,755,000
⇩ 4 years	−5%	−3%	−1%	−2%	+2%	−1%	−1%	−1%	−1%
1989	200,300	372,700	297,600	1,270,300	589,300	167,900	400,500	408,300	3,706,900
Percentage of total ⇨ %	5	10	8	34	16	5	11	11	100
Membership:									
1985	367,500	845,700	675,900	2,495,900	1,094,000	271,000	686,900	620,400	7,057,300
⇩ 4 years	−1%	0%	+1%	+3%	+3%	+4%	0%	−3%	+1%
1989	363,700	846,100	683,800	2,567,600	1,129,300	280,800	687,700	603,400	7,162,400
Percentage of total ⇨ %	5	12	9	36	16	4	10	8	100
Percentage ⇩ of churches in each category (vertical total 100%) whose **adult attendance** 1985-1989:									
Grew %	11	20	23	15	12	20	33	42	25
Remained static %	82	77	71	83	87	76	60	39	67
Declined %	7	3	6	2	1	4	7	19	8
Percentage ⇩ of churches in each category (vertical total 100%) in 1989 whose **services** were held:									
Morning only %	23	29	34	23	24	29	49	52	38
Morning & Evening %	69	64	58	74	74	67	42	24	51
Evening only %	8	7	8	3	2	4	9	24	11

Size of church by weekly adult attendance 1989[1]

	10 or under	11-25	26-50	51-100	101-150	151-200	201-300	301-400	401-500	Over 500	Average size[2]	Number (=100%)
Free Churches ⇨												
ALL Churches %	2	7	25	28	20	10	4	2	1	1	87	18,296
Growing churches %	0	2	7	28	32	17	8	3	2	1	123	4,467
Static churches %	2	9	34	27	14	7	3	2	1	1	75	12,357
Declining churches %	3	10	11	32	28	13	2	1	−	−	82	1,472
Anglicans												
ALL Churches %	4	15	24	22	16	11	6	1½	⌐ ½ ⌐		77	16,373
Growing churches %	0	3	14	24	25	19	9	3	1	1	117	4,582
Static churches %	6	18	29	22	12	7	5	1	−	−	62	10,642
Declining churches %	8	19	22	29	15	6	1	−	−	−	54	1,149
Roman Catholics												
ALL Churches %	1	1	1	2	7	13	14	14	10	37	355	3,824
Growing churches %	0	0	0	5	8	8	9	17	9	44	382	612
Static churches %	1	1	1	2	7	11	16	12	11	38	360	2,791
Declining churches %	0	0	6	0	9	19	21	21	8	16	282	421

[1] This table is based on responses from 65% of all the churches
[2] Total of morning and evening services (where both held) with those attending both times counted twice

Growth of Churches and Times of Services

	Methodist	Baptist	URC	Independent	Afro-Caribbean	Pentecostal	Other	TOTAL Free Churches	Anglican	Roman Catholic	TOTAL Christian
Percentage ⇩ of churches in each denomination (vertical total 100%) whose **adult attendance** 1985-1989:											
Grew %	16	33	21	29	29	35	18	24	28	16	25
Remained static %	73	61	70	66	64	58	73	68	65	73	67
Declined %	11	6	9	5	7	7	9	8	7	11	8
Percentage of churches which between 1975 and 1979:											
Grew %	8	21	12	25	7	38	16	15	23	11	18[1]
Percentage ⇩ of churches in each denomination (vertical total 100%) in 1989 whose **services** were held:											
Morning only %	26	12	40	32	10	7	36	26	49	39	38[2]
Morning & Evening %	50	80	51	58	84	87	52	60	44	57	51[2]
Evening only %	24	8	9	10	6	6	12	14	7	4	11[2]
Percentage ⇩ of 1989 **adult attenders** in each denomination (vertical total 100%) going:											
Morning only %	61	50	67	38	42	25	36	49	67	67	61[3]
Morning & Evening[4] %	18	31	14	31	41	48	37	28	10	4	14[3]
Evening only %	21	19	19	31	17	27	27	23	23	29	25[3]
Percentage of 1979 adult attenders in each denomination going in the:											
Morning[5] %	59	58	73	53	53	46	57	58	75	90	75

[1] Including Orthodox at 33%   [2] Respectively 31%, 56% and 13% for 1985   [3] Respectively 59%, 16% and 25% for 1985
[4] Twicers   [5] This line should be compared with the *total* of the top two of the preceding three lines

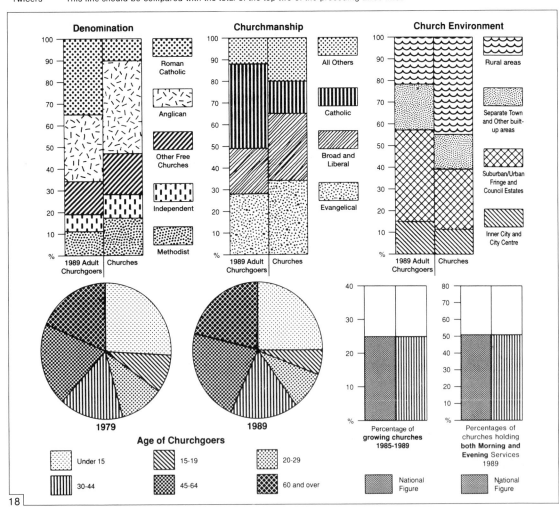

Churchmanship of church and people

Percentage of all churches 1989 ⇨ %	Broad Evan- gelical	Main- stream Evan- gelical	Charis- matic Evan- gelical	Total Evan- gelical	Low Church	Broad	Liberal	Anglo- Catholic	Catholic	All Others	ALL Churches
	7	16	11	34	12	17	14	6	15	2	100
Children attending:											
1985	117,900	141,900	194,200	454,000	74,000	108,900	120,100	40,500	470,100	13,300	1,280,900
⇩ 4 years	−10%	−9%	+3%	−4%	−8%	−6%	−5%	−4%	−4%	+2%	−5%
1989	106,200	128,700	199,900	434,800	67,900	102,200	113,500	38,700	450,900	13,500	1,221,500
Percentage of total ⇨ %	9	11	16	36	6	8	9	3	37	1	100
Adults attending:											
1985	349,100	256,500	394,800	1,000,400	243,500	389,800	426,500	169,600	1,466,300	58,900	3,755,000
⇩ 4 years	−3%	+2%	+7%	+3%	−4%	−5%	−4%	−5%	−2%	+3%	−1%
1989	340,300	262,800	424,100	1,027,200	233,700	369,900	409,900	161,500	1,444,200	60,500	3,706,900
Percentage of total ⇨ %	9	7	12	28	6	10	11	4	39	2	100
Membership:											
1985	416,000	283,600	398,400	1,098,000	309,800	511,500	555,300	230,800	4,054,300	297,600	7,057,300
⇩ 4 years	−2%	+2%	+6%	+2%	−3%	−4%	−3%	−5%	+3%	+2%	+1%
1989	406,400	288,100	420,400	1,114,900	300,800	493,400	536,900	219,400	4,193,300	303,700	7,162,400
Percentage of total ⇨ %	6	4	6	16	4	7	7	3	59	4	100
Percentage ⇩ of churches in each category (vertical total 100%) whose **adult attendance** 1985-1989:											
Grew %	24	26	41	30	20	23	24	25	21	18	25
Remained static %	72	62	52	63	71	68	68	68	71	73	67
Declined %	4	12	7	7	9	9	8	7	8	9	8
Percentage ⇩ of churches in each category (vertical total 100%) whose **services** were held:											
Morning only %	43	41	30	38	49	52	35	43	17	22	38
Morning & Evening %	44	55	62	55	37	33	51	47	71	71	51
Evening only %	13	4	8	7	14	15	14	10	12	7	11

Year church/congregation founded

	Before 1500	1500- 1799	1800- 1849	1850- 1874	1875- 1899	1900- 1924	1925- 1949	1950- 1974	1975 or later	ALL Churches
Percentage of all churches 1989 ⇨%	24	7	12	12	14	8	8	9	6	100
Percentage ⇩ of churches in each category (vertical total 100%) in 1989 which were:										
Free Church %	1[1]	65	57	45	62	57	58	55	90	47
Anglican %	99	25	36	44	30	31	21	22	7	43
Catholic %	0	10	7	11	8	12	21	23	3	10
Percentage ⇩ of churches in each category (vertical total 100%) whose **adult attendance** 1985-1989:										
Grew %	28	23	26	23	23	22	24	27	44	25
Remained static %	66	71	66	70	68	70	69	64	50	67
Declined %	6	6	8	7	9	8	7	9	6	8

[1] Residential schools/colleges

Types of Third World Community Aid church would support

Percentage of all churches 1989 ⇨ %	Project activities	Specific Geographical area	Named communities	Named individuals	Administered through local churches	Evangelism/ missionary work	Other	No support	TOTAL ALL Churches
	42	19	12	17	38	54	1	2	185[1]
Percentage ⇩ of churches in each category (vertical total 100%) whose **adult attendance** 1985-1989:									
Grew %	26	27	26	29	26	27	22	18	25
Remained static %	67	64	66	63	66	66	71	71	67
Declined %	7	9	8	8	8	7	7	11	8
Percentage ⇩ of churches in each category (vertical total 100%) whose **services** were held:									
Morning only %	40	43	46	35	37	31	60	59	38
Morning & Evening %	49	49	47	56	50	58	17	15	51
Evening only %	11	8	7	9	13	11	23	26	11

[1] This number is greater than 100% because multiple answers were possible

THE FUTURE
All England, if present trends continue

Estimated total adult population 2000: 39,535,000

Change 1989-2000: +2%

Estimated total child population 2000: 10,039,000

Change 1989-2000: +13%

2000 adult church attendance as percentage of adult population: 9%

2000 child church attendance as percentage of child population: 11%

Adult and Church Attenders and Membership

Attenders Percentage of all churches 2000 ⇨ %	Metho- dist	Baptist	URC	Inde- pendent	Afro- Carib- bean	Pente- costal	Other	TOTAL Free Churches	Anglican	Roman Catholic	TOTAL Christian[2]
	15	6	4	14	3	3	4	49	40	11	100
Attenders											
Children											
1989	116,200	71,500	35,300	132,700	35,600	37,400	30,600	459,300	348,000	411,300	1,221,500
⇩ 11 years	−39%	−21%	−38%	+28%	−11%	+18%	−28%	−9%	−14%	−10%	−11%
2000	71,400	56,800	21,800	169,700	31,700	44,300	22,100	417,800	299,400	370,600	1,091,300
Percentage of total ⇨ %	6	5	2	16	3	4	2	38	28	34	100
Average children attending **1989**	17	31	21	32	38	37	21	25	21	108	32
2000	12	23	14	31	32	40	15	22	19	88	28
Adults											
1989	396,100	199,400	114,000	292,800	68,500	95,200	83,000	1,249,000	1,143,900	1,304,600	3,706,900
⇩ 11 years	−11%	+3%	−20%	+36%	+2%	+25%	−12%	+5%	−11%	−15%	−7%
2000	352,000	205,000	91,000	397,000	70,000	119,000	73,000	1,307,000	1,017,000	1,112,000	3,448,000
Percentage of total ⇨ %	10	6	3	11	2	4	2	38	30	32	100
Average adults attending[1] **1989**	59	85	68	71	72	95	57	68	70	341	96
2000	60	84	59	71	73	108	49	69	65	265	88

Membership	Metho- dist	Baptist	URC	Inde- pendent	Afro- Carib- bean	Pente- costal	Other	TOTAL Free Churches	Anglican	Roman Catholic[3]	TOTAL Christian[2]
1989	422,200	170,600	119,900	222,100	68,200	68,000	103,200	1,174,200	1,559,000	4,197,100	7,162,400
⇩ 11 years	−10%	+17%	−9%	+36%	+23%	+28%	−12%	+7%	−16%	+3%	0%
2000	378,100	199,500	109,400	302,500	84,000	87,000	90,800	1,251,300	1,308,800	4,337,100	7,153,600
Percentage of total ⇨ %	5	3	2	4	1	1	1	17	18	61	100
Members per church **1979**	63	73	71	51	105	72	66	64	95	1,037	186
2000	64	81	71	55	84	79	61	66	84	1,033	183
Number of Churches **1989**	6,740	2,339	1,681	4,123	949	1,002	1,462	18,296	16,373	3,824	38,607
2000	5,900	2,450	1,550	5,550	1,000	1,100	1,500	19,050	15,600	4,200	39,000

[1] Sunday morning and evening adult congregations combined (where both held), excluding twicers

[2] This column includes Orthodox Church figures of child attendance of 2,900 and 3,500; adult attendance figures of 9,400, and 12,000, and membership figures of 232,100, and 256,400 for 1989 and 2000 respectively with 114 congregations in 1989 and 150 in 2000

[3] Membership figures are Roman Catholic population

Age and sex of churchgoers 1989 and 2000

Age-Group	Population 1989			Churchgoers in 1989			Churchgoers in 2000			Population 2000		
	Men %	Women %	Total %	Men %	Women %	Total %	Men %	Women %	Total %	Men %	Women %	Total %
Under 15	10	9	19	12	13	25	11	12	23	10	10	20
15-19	4	4	8	3	4	7	2	5	7	3	3	6
20-29	8	8	16	4	6	10	3	6	9	6	6	12
30-44	10	10	20	7	10	17	7	11	18	11	11	22
45-64	11	11	22	9	13	22	9	14	23	12	12	24
65 and over	6	9	15	7	12	19	8	12	20	7	9	16
All ages	49	51	100	42	58	100	40	60	100	49	51	100

Church environment

Children attending:	City Centre	Inner City	Council Estate	Suburban/Urban Fringe	Separate Town	Other built-up area	Rural area: Commuter dormitory	Rural area: Other	ALL England
1989	46,300	106,400	99,700	437,000	188,800	57,600	163,000	122,700	1,221,500
11 years	−17%	+1%	−7%	−13%	−11%	+5%	−11%	−20%	−11%
2000	38,500	107,700	92,600	381,600	167,200	60,200	145,800	97,700	1,091,300
Percentage of total %	4	10	8	35	15	6	13	9	100
Adults attending:									
1989	200,300	372,700	297,600	1,270,300	589,300	167,900	400,500	408,300	3,706,900
11 years	−16%	−14%	−9%	−8%	−1%	−1%	−4%	−6%	−7%
2000	169,000	320,000	272,000	1,171,000	583,000	166,000	384,000	383,000	3,448,000
Percentage of total %	5	9	8	34	17	5	11	11	100
Membership:									
1989	363,700	846,100	683,800	2,567,600	1,129,300	280,800	687,700	603,400	7,162,400
11 years	−7%	−4%	−1%	+3%	+4%	+6%	−4%	−11%	0%
2000	338,400	811,000	675,800	2,656,800	1,179,700	296,400	660,400	535,100	7,153,600
Percentage of total %	5	11	9	37	17	4	9	8	100

Churchmanship

Children attending:	Broad Evangelical	Mainstream Evangelical	Charismatic Evangelical	Total Evangelical	Low Church	Broad	Liberal	Anglo-Catholic	Catholic	All Others	ALL Churchmanships
1989	106,200	128,700	199,900	434,800	67,900	102,200	113,500	38,700	450,900	13,500	1,221,500
11 years	−25%	−24%	+8%	−10%	−20%	−15%	−13%	−10%	−9%	+6%	−11%
2000	79,300	97,900	215,500	392,700	54,500	87,300	98,900	34,800	408,800	14,300	1,091,300
Percentage of total %	7	9	20	36	5	8	9	3	38	1	100
Adults attending:											
1989	340,300	262,800	424,700	1,027,200	233,700	369,900	409,900	161,500	1,444,200	60,500	3,706,900
11 years	−10%	−5%	+17%	+2%	−7%	−11%	−12%	−14%	−10%	−6%	−7%
2000	305,000	249,000	497,000	1,051,000	218,000	328,000	361,000	139,000	1,294,000	57,000	3,448,000
Percentage of total %	9	7	14	30	6	10	11	4	37	2	100
Membership:											
1989	406,400	288,100	420,400	1,114,900	300,800	493,400	536,900	219,400	4,193,300	303,700	7,162,400
11 years	−11%	−1%	+10%	0%	−12%	−13%	−13%	−17%	+5%	+1%	0%
2000	362,000	285,700	462,900	1,110,600	265,000	426,900	467,500	182,400	4,394,500	306,700	7,153,600
Percentage of total %	5	4	6	15	4	6	7	3	61	4	100

Regions

Children attending:	North	Yorks/Humberside	North West	East Midlands	West Midlands	East Anglia	South East (North)	South East (Greater London)	South East (South)	South West	ALL England
1989	75,800	110,000	211,300	90,700	126,300	58,000	124,700	158,900	141,400	124,400	1,221,500
11 years	−8%	−18%	−9%	−18%	−17%	−15%	−20%	+2%	−4%	−10%	−11%
2000	69,900	90,100	192,400	74,800	104,500	49,100	99,900	162,700	135,600	112,300	1,091,300
Percentage of total %	6	8	18	7	10	4	9	15	13	10	100
Adults attending:											
1989	248,700	336,800	607,000	255,300	410,200	177,500	339,900	502,500	429,100	399,900	3,706,900
11 years	−10%	−8%	−15%	−10%	0%	0%	−9%	−5%	−6%	−3%	−7%
2000	223,000	309,000	518,000	230,000	409,000	178,000	311,000	478,000	404,000	388,000	3,448,000
Percentage of total %	6	9	15	7	12	5	9	14	12	11	100
Membership:											
1989	539,600	648,200	1,486,500	431,800	821,000	268,600	642,300	1,054,700	699,500	570,200	7,162,400
11 years	−7%	−2%	+3%	−2%	+5%	+5%	+1%	+4%	−7%	−9%	0%
2000	502,800	637,200	1,528,500	424,900	862,700	281,100	646,800	1,097,400	650,600	521,600	7,153,600
Percentage of total %	7	9	22	6	12	4	9	15	9	7	100

METHODISTS

1989 Methodist adult church attendance as percentage of adult population: **1.0%**

1989 Methodist adult church attendance as percentage of all adult church attendance: **11%**

1989 Methodist child church attendance as percentage of child population: **1.3%**

1989 Methodist child church attendance as percentage of all child church attendance: **10%**

Percentage of churches responding: **76%**

Churchmanship of church and people

Percentage of all churches 1989 ⇨ %	Broad Evan-gelical	Main-stream Evan-gelical	Charis-matic Evan-gelical	Total Evan-gelical	Low Church	Broad	Liberal	Anglo-Catholic	Catholic	All Others	ALL Churches
1989 ⇨ %	*22*	*7*	*4*	*33*	*24*	*23*	*16*	*0*	*1*	*3*	*100*
Children attending:											
1985	33,600	10,100	9,000	52,700	25,600	31,500	24,900	200	500	2,700	138,100
⇩ 4 years	−15%	−13%	−8%	−13%	−19%	−16%	−18%	−50%	0%	−15%	−16%
1989	28,500	8,800	8,300	45,600	20,800	26,400	20,500	100	500	2,300	116,200
Percentage of total ⇨ %	*24*	*8*	*7*	*39*	*18*	*23*	*18*	*0*	*0*	*2*	*100*
Adults attending:											
1985	100,500	16,400	16,300	133,200	74,800	113,400	85,900	500	4,000	9,000	420,800
⇩ 4 years	−7%	+2%	−7%	−5%	+2%	−15%	−5%	0%	+35%	−1%	−6%
1989	93,900	16,800	15,200	125,900	76,600	96,900	81,900	500	5,400	8,900	396,100
Percentage of total ⇨ %	*24*	*4*	*4*	*32*	*19*	*25*	*21*	*0*	*1*	*2*	*100*
Membership:											
1985	97,500	41,200	22,300	161,000	81,700	97,400	81,300	400	4,000	10,000	435,800
⇩ 4 years	−4%	−19%	+6%	−6%	−5%	0%	0%	0%	+18%	−2%	−3%
1989	93,900	33,200	23,600	150,700	78,000	97,200	81,400	400	4,700	9,800	422,200
Percentage of total ⇨ %	*22*	*8*	*6*	*36*	*19*	*23*	*19*	*0*	*1*	*2*	*100*
Percentage ⇩ of churches in each category (vertical total 100%) whose **adult attendance** 1985-1989:											
Grew %	*18*	*9*	*24*	*18*	*13*	*15*	*17*	—	*(29)*	*9*	*16*
Remained static %	*75*	*79*	*64*	*73*	*77*	*71*	*71*	—	*(50)*	*76*	*73*
Declined %	*7*	*12*	*12*	*9*	*10*	*14*	*12*	—	*(21)*	*15*	*11*

Year church/congregation founded

	Before 1500	1500-1799	1800-1849	1850-1874	1875-1899	1900-1924	1925-1949	1950-1974	1975 or later	ALL Churches
Percentage of all churches 1989 ⇨ %	*0*	*5*	*22*	*22*	*24*	*13*	*5*	*7*	*2*	*100*
Percentage ⇩ of churches in each category (vertical total 100%) whose **adult attendance** 1985-1989:										
Grew %	—	16	17	15	18	16	10	14	32	16
Remained static %	—	69	73	78	74	71	78	68	49	73
Declined %	—	15	10	7	8	13	12	18	19	11

Types of Third World Community Aid church would support

Percentage of all churches 1989 ⇨ %	Project activities	Specific Geographical area	Named communities	Named individuals	Administered through local churches	Evangelism/ missionary work	Other	No support	TOTAL ALL Churches
Percentage of all churches 1989 ⇨ %	*37*	*12*	*8*	*14*	*52*	*60*	*1*	*1*	*185[1]*
Percentage ⇩ of churches in each category (vertical total 100%) whose **adult attendance** 1985-1989:									
Grew %	17	17	12	21	16	16	17	17	16
Remained static %	71	73	74	68	73	74	70	74	73
Declined %	12	10	14	11	11	10	13	9	11

[1] Figures sum to more than *100%* because multiple answers were possible

Age and sex of churchgoers 1979 and 1989

Age-Group	Population 1979			Churchgoers in 1979			Churchgoers in 1989[1]			Population 1989		
	Men %	Women %	Total %	Men %	Women %	Total %	Men %	Women %	Total %	Men %	Women %	Total %
Under 15	11	10	21	14	14	28	9	14	23	10	9	19
15-19	4	4	8	2	3	5	2	3	5	4	4	8
20-29	7	7	14	2	3	5	3	4	7	8	8	16
30-44	10	9	19	5	7	12	5	7	12	10	10	20
45-64	11	12	23	8	17	25	8	15	23	11	11	22
65 and over	6	9	15	9	16	25	10	20	30	6	9	15
All ages	49	51	100	40	60	100	37	63	100	49	51	100

[1] This table is based on responses from 64% of all Methodist churches in England

Church environment

Percentage of all churches 1989 %	City Centre 2	Inner City 5	Council Estate 5	Suburban/ Urban Fringe 21	Separate Town 11	Other built-up area 5	Rural area: Commuter dormitory 13	Rural area: Other 38	ALL Churches 100
Children attending:									
1985	2,000	3,600	8,600	49,300	21,400	5,400	17,900	29,900	138,100
🡣 4 years	−15%	−25%	−35%	−9%	−4%	−2%	−16%	−31%	−16%
1989	1,700	2,700	5,600	44,800	20,600	5,300	15,000	20,500	116,200
Percentage of total 🡢 %	1	2	5	38	18	5	13	18	100
Adults attending:									
1985	14,800	23,000	18,600	143,800	77,600	22,000	46,400	74,600	420,800
🡣 4 years	−4%	−3%	−8%	−6%	−9%	0%	−10%	−2%	−6%
1989	14,200	22,200	17,200	135,200	70,900	22,000	41,700	72,700	396,100
Percentage of total 🡢 %	4	6	4	34	18	6	10	18	100
Membership:									
1985	14,700	22,800	17,000	147,900	81,900	23,300	52,800	75,400	435,800
🡣 4 years	+1%	−3%	−2%	−2%	−4%	−5%	−10%	−1%	−3%
1989	14,800	22,200	16,600	145,100	78,900	22,200	47,400	75,000	422,200
Percentage of total 🡢 %	4	5	4	34	19	5	11	18	100
Percentage 🡣 of churches in each category (vertical total 100%) whose **adult attendance** 1985-1989:									
Grew %	25	11	8	18	24	16	13	12	16
Remained static %	44	70	86	70	61	75	80	83	73
Declined %	31	19	6	12	15	9	7	5	11
Percentage 🡣 of churches in each category (vertical total 100%) in 1985 whose **services** were held:									
Morning only %	15	10	22	12	8	24	33	30	22
Morning & Evening %	73	86	63	81	90	62	52	31	58
Evening only %	12	4	15	7	2	14	15	39	20
Percentage 🡣 of churches in each category (vertical total 100%) in 1989 whose **services** were held:									
Morning only %	12	15	25	18	17	22	39	31	26
Morning & Evening %	74	76	56	74	78	67	46	23	50
Evening only %	14	9	19	8	5	11	15	46	24

Size[1] of church by weekly adult attendance 1979 and 1989[2]

	10 or under	11-25	26-50	51- 100	101- 150	151- 200	201- 300	301- 400	401- 500	Over 500	Average size[1]	Number (=100%)
ALL Churches 1979 %	5	27	23	19	15	5	6	—	—	—	59	7,636
ALL Churches 1989 %	2	19	30	22	13	6	5	2	1	—	70	6,740
Growing churches[3] %	0	15	20	35	14	5	6	3	1	1	83	1,091
Static churches[3] %	1	21	35	16	12	7	5	2	1	—	69	4,908
Declining churches[3] %	11	17	8	44	14	5	1	—	—	—	55	741

[1] Total of morning and evening services (when both held) with those attending both times counted twice
[2] This table is based on responses from 72% of all Methodist churches in 1989   [3] 1989 figures

BAPTISTS

1989 Baptist adult church attendance as percentage of adult population: **0.5%**

1989 Baptist adult church attendance as percentage of all adult church attendance: **5%**

1989 Baptist child church attendance as percentage of child population: **0.8%**

1989 Baptist child church attendance as percentage of all child church attendance: **6%**

Percentage of churches responding: **73%**

Churchmanship of church and people

Percentage of all churches	Broad Evan-gelical	Main-stream Evan-gelical	Charis-matic Evan-gelical	Total Evan-gelical	Low Church	Broad	Liberal	Anglo-Catholic	Catholic	All Others	ALL Churches
1989 ⇨ %	*19*	*42*	*23*	*84*	*5*	*5*	*5*	*0*	*0*	*1*	*100*
Children attending:											
1985	13,900	33,500	23,700	71,100	2,400	2,300	2,000	0	100	300	78,200
⇩ *4 years*	*−15%*	*−11%*	*−2%*	*−9%*	*−8%*	*−4%*	*−5%*	*−*	*0%*	*0%*	*−9%*
1989	11,800	29,800	23,200	64,800	2,200	2,200	1,900	0	100	300	71,500
Percentage of total ⇨ %	*17*	*42*	*32*	*91*	*3*	*3*	*3*	*0*	*0*	*0*	*100*
Adults attending:											
1985	42,700	75,300	39,000	157,000	6,800	12,700	18,200	100	400	1,000	196,200
⇩ *4 years*	*−12%*	*+5%*	*+13%*	*+2%*	*+4%*	*−2%*	*−2%*	*0%*	*+25%*	*0%*	*+2%*
1989	37,400	79,200	43,900	160,500	7,100	12,400	17,800	100	500	1,000	199,400
Percentage of total ⇨ %	*19*	*39*	*22*	*80*	*4*	*6*	*9*	*0*	*0*	*1*	*100*
Membership:											
1985	36,500	61,800	47,600	145,900	5,300	5,500	7,300	100	1,700	1,000	166,800
⇩ *4 years*	*−3%*	*+1%*	*+9%*	*+3%*	*+4%*	*−5%*	*−1%*	*0%*	*+18%*	*−10%*	*+2%*
1989	35,400	62,200	52,100	149,700	5,500	5,200	7,200	100	2,000	900	170,600
Percentage of total ⇨ %	*21*	*36*	*31*	*88*	*3*	*3*	*4*	*0*	*1*	*1*	*100*
Percentage ⇩ of churches in each category (vertical total 100%) whose **adult attendance** 1985-1989:											
Grew %	*24*	*37*	*47*	*35*	*26*	*22*	*17*	*−*	*−*	*(20)*	*33*
Remained static %	*73*	*51*	*47*	*59*	*69*	*70*	*78*	*−*	*−*	*(80)*	*61*
Declined %	*3*	*12*	*6*	*6*	*5*	*8*	*5*	*−*	*−*	*(0)*	*6*

Year church/congregation founded

	Before 1500	1500-1799	1800-1849	1850-1874	1875-1899	1900-1924	1925-1949	1950-1974	1975 or later	ALL Churches
Percentage of all churches 1989 ⇨%	*0*	*16*	*25*	*14*	*16*	*8*	*8*	*7*	*6*	*100*
Percentage ⇩ of churches in each category (vertical total 100%) whose **adult attendance** 1985-1989:										
Grew %	*−*	*29*	*34*	*25*	*32*	*35*	*37*	*38*	*38*	*33*
Remained static %	*−*	*67*	*61*	*69*	*61*	*57*	*58*	*53*	*57*	*61*
Declined %	*−*	*4*	*5*	*6*	*7*	*8*	*5*	*9*	*5*	*6*

Types of Third World Community Aid church would support

Percentage of all churches 1989 ⇨ %	Project activities	Specific Geographical area	Named communities	Named individuals	Administered through local churches	Evangelism/ missionary work	Other	No support	TOTAL ALL Churches
	44	*14*	*5*	*18*	*29*	*84*	*1*	*2*	*197*[1]
Percentage ⇩ of churches in each category (vertical total 100%) whose **adult attendance** 1985-1989:									
Grew %	*31*	*35*	*33*	*43*	*37*	*33*	*(0)*	*18*	*33*
Remained static %	*62*	*52*	*60*	*52*	*57*	*61*	*(100)*	*71*	*61*
Declined %	*7*	*13*	*7*	*5*	*6*	*6*	*(0)*	*11*	*6*

[1] Figures sum to more than *100%* because multiple answers were possible

Age and sex of churchgoers 1979 and 1989

Age-Group	Population 1979			Churchgoers in 1979			Churchgoers in 1989[1]			Population 1989		
	Men %	Women %	Total %	Men %	Women %	Total %	Men %	Women %	Total %	Men %	Women %	Total %
Under 15	11	10	21	14	16	30	12	14	26	10	9	19
15-19	4	4	8	3	5	8	3	4	7	4	4	8
20-29	7	7	14	5	4	9	5	5	10	8	8	16
30-44	10	9	19	7	9	16	7	11	18	10	10	20
45-64	11	12	23	7	12	19	7	13	20	11	11	22
65 and over	6	9	15	7	11	18	6	13	19	6	9	15
All ages	49	51	100	43	57	100	40	60	100	49	51	100

[1] This table is based on responses from 67% of all Baptist churches in England

Church environment

Percentage of all churches 1989 %	City Centre 3	Inner City 8	Council Estate 6	Suburban/ Urban Fringe 29	Separate Town 16	Other built-up area 5	Rural area: Commuter dormitory 14	Rural area: Other 19	ALL Churches 100
Children attending:									
1985	1,100	2,800	3,000	30,700	18,300	4,400	11,300	6,600	78,200
⇩ 4 years	+9%	−14%	+3%	−3%	−10%	−25%	−19%	−9%	−9%
1989	1,200	2,400	3,100	29,900	16,400	3,300	9,200	6,000	71,500
Percentage of total ⇨ %	2	3	4	42	23	5	13	8	100
Adults attending:									
1985	6,600	15,300	6,400	74,500	45,300	8,300	23,500	16,300	196,200
⇩ 4 years	+8%	−4%	+11%	+1%	+4%	+11%	−5%	+3%	+2%
1989	7,100	14,700	7,100	75,100	47,000	9,200	22,400	16,800	199,400
Percentage of total ⇨ %	4	7	4	38	23	5	11	8	100
Membership:									
1985	6,400	11,500	5,100	65,000	44,500	7,200	16,400	10,700	166,800
⇩ 4 years	−3%	0%	−2%	+3%	−2%	+10%	+9%	+7%	+2%
1989	6,200	11,500	5,000	66,800	43,800	7,900	17,900	11,500	170,600
Percentage of total ⇨ %	4	7	3	39	25	5	10	7	100
Percentage ⇩ of churches in each category (vertical total 100%) whose **adult attendance** 1985-1989:									
Grew %	28	41	36	30	40	35	33	23	33
Remained static %	60	48	60	64	53	58	63	73	61
Declined %	12	11	4	6	7	7	4	4	6
Percentage ⇩ of churches in each category (vertical total 100%) in 1985 whose **services** were held:									
Morning only %	23	10	13	3	8	25	10	19	10
Morning & Evening %	67	86	82	96	89	80	81	60	83
Evening only %	10	4	5	1	3	5	9	21	7
Percentage ⇩ of churches in each category (vertical total 100%) in 1989 whose **services** were held:									
Morning only %	27	19	15	3	5	16	17	21	12
Morning & Evening %	62	77	79	96	93	78	76	53	80
Evening only %	11	4	6	1	2	6	7	26	8

Size[1] of church by weekly adult attendance 1979 and 1989[2]

	10 or under	11-25	26-50	51-100	101-150	151-200	201-300	301-400	401-500	Over 500	Average size[1]	Number (=100%)
ALL Churches 1979 %	6	11	26	25	11	5	8	5	2	1	92	2,211
ALL Churches 1989 %	4	9	15	25	18	12	8	5	3	1	112	2,339
Growing churches[3] %	0	8	9	30	18	13	9	8	3	2	137	772
Static churches[3] %	5	10	23	21	14	10	8	4	4	1	106	1,427
Declining churches[3] %	9	11	9	41	20	4	5	1	−	−	70	140

[1] Total of morning and evening services (when both held) with those attending both times counted twice
[2] This table is based on responses from 70% of all Baptist churches in 1989   [3] 1989 figures

UNITED REFORMED CHURCH

1989 URC adult church attendance as percentage of adult population: 0.3%

1989 URC adult church attendance as percentage of all adult church attendance: 3%

1989 URC child church attendance as percentage of child population: 0.4%

1989 URC child church attendance as percentage of all child church attendance: 3%

Percentage of churches responding: 77%

Churchmanship of church and people

Percentage of all churches	Broad Evan-gelical	Main-stream Evan-gelical	Charis-matic Evan-gelical	Total Evan-gelical	Low Church	Broad	Liberal	Anglo-Catholic	Catholic	All Others	ALL Churches
1989 ⇨ %	16	4	4	24	17	19	37	0	0	3	100
Children attending:											
1985	3,000	2,000	5,700	10,700	6,800	7,400	16,900	0	200	700	42,700
⇩ 4 years	−37%	−25%	−9%	−19%	−24%	−11%	−17%	—	0%	−14%	−17%
1989	1,900	1,600	5,200	8,700	5,200	6,600	14,000	0	200	600	35,300
Percentage of total ⇨ %	5	4	15	24	15	19	40	0	0	2	100
Adults attending:											
1985	3,800	2,700	5,900	12,400	19,300	25,500	61,300	0	700	2,200	121,400
⇩ 4 years	−5%	−11%	+24%	+7%	−9%	−2%	−11%	—	+71%	+9%	−6%
1989	3,600	2,400	7,300	13,300	17,500	25,000	54,600	0	1,200	2,400	114,000
Percentage of total ⇨ %	3	2	7	12	15	22	48	0	1	2	100
Membership:											
1985	20,900	2,000	5,100	28,000	17,500	23,400	53,900	0	2,000	2,400	127,200
⇩ 4 years	+1%	0%	+4%	+1%	−7%	−8%	−9%	—	0%	0%	−6%
1989	21,100	2,000	5,300	28,400	16,300	21,600	49,200	0	2,000	2,400	119,900
Percentage of total ⇨ %	18	2	4	24	13	18	41	0	2	2	100
Percentage ⇩ of churches in each category (vertical total 100%) whose **adult attendance** 1985-1989:											
Grew %	28	33	28	28	13	26	17	—	—	(25)	21
Remained static %	64	67	63	65	77	65	72	—	—	(75)	70
Declined %	8	0	9	7	10	9	11	—	—	(0)	9

Year church/congregation founded

	Before 1500	1500-1799	1800-1849	1850-1874	1875-1899	1900-1924	1925-1949	1950-1974	1975 or later	ALL Churches
Percentage of all churches 1989 ⇨ %	0	25	20	14	15	8	8	8	2	100
Percentage ⇩ of churches in each category (vertical total 100%) whose **adult attendance** 1985-1989:										
Grew %	—	28	19	22	24	10	16	23	16	21
Remained static %	—	67	73	70	61	80	77	61	72	70
Declined %	—	5	8	8	15	10	7	16	12	9

Types of Third World Community Aid church would support

Percentage of all churches 1989 ⇨ %	Project activities	Specific Geographical area	Named communities	Named individuals	Administered through local churches	Evangelism/ missionary work	Other	No support	TOTAL ALL Churches
	58	16	11	20	40	37	1	1	184[1]
Percentage ⇩ of churches in each category (vertical total 100%) whose **adult attendance** 1985-1989:									
Grew %	22	27	31	24	19	21	(33)	(20)	21
Remained static %	70	62	62	61	73	71	(61)	(60)	70
Declined %	8	11	7	15	8	8	(6)	(20)	9

[1] Figures sum to more than *100%* because multiple answers were possible

Age and sex of churchgoers 1979 and 1989

Age-Group	Population 1979			Churchgoers in 1979[1]			Churchgoers in 1989[2]			Population 1989		
	Men %	Women %	Total %	Men %	Women %	Total %	Men %	Women %	Total %	Men %	Women %	Total %
Under 15	11	10	21	15	12	27	11	13	24	10	9	19
15-19	4	4	8	2	3	5	2	2	4	4	4	8
20-29	7	7	14	3	4	7	2	4	6	8	8	16
30-44	10	9	19	6	8	14	5	8	13	10	10	20
45-64	11	12	23	9	12	21	8	15	23	11	11	22
65 and over	6	9	15	8	18	26	9	21	30	6	9	15
All ages	49	51	100	43	57	100	37	63	100	49	51	100

[1] These figures include attendance at a small number of congregational churches. In 1989 these are included in the Independent tables
[2] This table is based on responses from 70% of all URC churches in England

Church environment

Percentage of all churches 1989 %	City Centre	Inner City	Council Estate	Suburban/ Urban Fringe	Separate Town	Other built-up area	Rural area: Commuter dormitory	Rural area: Other	ALL Churches
	3	7	4	33	20	5	12	16	100
Children attending:									
1985	800	1,000	1,000	19,300	11,100	2,300	3,900	3,300	42,700
⇩ 4 years	+13%	−20%	+10%	−25%	−3%	−22%	−21%	−30%	−17%
1989	900	800	1,100	14,500	10,800	1,800	3,100	2,300	35,300
Percentage of total ⇨ %	2	2	3	41	31	5	9	7	100
Adults attending:									
1985	3,700	6,400	2,600	54,200	25,900	5,800	11,400	11,400	121,400
⇩ 4 years	+19%	−11%	+31%	−11%	0%	+14%	−9%	−18%	−6%
1989	4,400	5,700	3,400	48,400	25,800	6,600	10,400	9,300	114,000
Percentage of total ⇨ %	4	5	3	42	23	6	9	8	100
Membership:									
1985	3,800	5,900	4,900	53,500	28,000	7,600	10,300	13,200	127,200
⇩ 4 years	+11%	−8%	0%	−11%	0%	+13%	−4%	−12%	−6%
1989	4,200	5,400	4,900	47,400	27,900	8,600	9,900	11,600	119,900
Percentage of total ⇨ %	3	5	4	40	23	7	8	10	100
Percentage ⇩ of churches in each category (vertical total 100%) whose **adult attendance** 1985-1989:									
Grew %	30	30	14	19	24	29	50	5	21
Remained static %	50	55	76	71	69	67	35	90	70
Declined %	20	15	10	10	7	4	15	5	9
Percentage ⇩ of churches in each category (vertical total 100%) in 1985 whose **services** were held:									
Morning only %	41	16	43	31	33	40	50	13	33
Morning & Evening %	55	83	44	67	63	56	44	64	59
Evening only %	4	1	13	2	4	4	6	23	8
Percentage ⇩ of churches in each category (vertical total 100%) in 1989 whose **services** were held:									
Morning only %	58	32	51	36	38	61	51	19	40
Morning & Evening %	34	64	32	61	57	31	40	44	51
Evening only %	8	4	17	3	5	8	9	37	9

Size[1] of church by weekly adult attendance 1979 and 1989[2]

	10 or under	11-25	26-50	51-100	101-150	151-200	201-300	301-400	401-500	Over 500	Average size[1]	Number (=100%)
ALL Churches 1979 %	2	12	27	24	16	13	5	1	—	—	76	1,829
ALL Churches 1989 %	1	17	24	25	12	12	7	2	—	—	77	1,681
Growing churches[3] %	0	8	17	30	18	14	8	3	1	—	97	353
Static churches[3] %	2	20	28	22	9	12	7	2	—	—	75	1,177
Declining churches[3] %	0	14	8	59	16	2	1	—	—	—	60	151

[1] Total of morning and evening services (when both held) with those attending both times counted twice
[2] This table is based on responses from 66% of all URC churches in 1989   [3] 1989 figures

INDEPENDENTS

1989 Independent adult church attendance
as percentage of adult population: 0.8%

1989 Independent adult church attendance
as percentage of all adult church attendance: 8%

1989 Independent child church attendance
as percentage of child population: 1.5%

1989 Independent child church attendance
as percentage of all child church attendance: 11%

Percentage of churches responding: 58%

Churchmanship of church and people

Percentage of all churches 1989 ⇨ %	Broad Evan-gelical	Main-stream Evan-gelical	Charis-matic Evan-gelical	Total Evan-gelical	Low Church	Broad	Liberal	Anglo-Catholic	Catholic	All Others	ALL Churches
	4	38	37	79	4	4	6	2	3	2	100
Children attending:											
1985	3,200	52,000	43,300	98,500	4,300	4,700	7,000	1,700	1,000	1,400	118,600
⇩ 4 years	+19%	−6%	+25%	+9%	+21%	+36%	+7%	+94%	+40%	+43%	+12%
1989	3,800	48,900	54,200	106,900	5,200	6,400	7,500	3,300	1,400	2,000	132,700
Percentage of total ⇨ %	3	37	41	81	4	5	6	2	1	1	100
Adults attending:											
1985	31,500	64,700	96,700	192,900	6,700	15,500	14,500	14,900	10,000	3,000	257,500
⇩ 4 years	0%	−1%	+19%	+9%	+22%	+25%	+17%	+17%	+47%	+73%	+14%
1989	31,600	64,300	115,200	211,100	8,200	19,300	16,900	17,400	14,700	5,200	292,800
Percentage of total ⇨ %	11	22	39	72	3	6	6	6	5	2	100
Membership:											
1985	10,500	51,900	61,800	124,200	7,100	21,900	18,200	12,200	11,000	4,000	198,600
⇩ 4 years	+67%	+19%	+27%	+27%	+6%	−40%	+1%	−33%	+5%	+40%	+12%
1989	17,500	61,700	78,500	157,700	7,500	13,200	18,300	8,200	11,600	5,600	222,100
Percentage of total ⇨ %	8	28	35	71	3	6	8	4	5	3	100
Percentage ⇩ of churches in each category (vertical total 100%) whose **adult attendance** 1985-1989:											
Grew %	20	26	46	35	28	(29)	24	(30)	25	(24)	33
Remained static %	79	72	48	61	65	(71)	71	(70)	65	(76)	63
Declined %	1	2	6	4	7	(0)	5	(0)	10	(0)	4

Year church/congregation founded

	Before 1500	1500-1799	1800-1849	1850-1874	1875-1899	1900-1924	1925-1949	1950-1974	1975 or later	ALL Churches
Percentage of all churches 1989 ⇨ %	1[1]	5	7	7	13	10	13	14	30	100
Percentage ⇩ of churches in each category (vertical total 100%) whose **adult attendance** 1985-1989:										
Grew %	21	30	20	15	21	23	23	34	57	29
Remained static %	73	67	73	81	73	72	72	61	39	66
Declined %	6	3	7	4	6	5	5	5	4	5

[1] All residential schools/colleges

Types of Third World Community Aid church would support

Percentage of all churches 1989 ⇨ %	Project activities	Specific Geographical area	Named communities	Named individuals	Administered through local churches	Evangelism/ missionary work	Other	No support	TOTAL ALL Churches
	28	18	9	23	31	73	1	2	185[1]
Percentage ⇩ of churches in each category (vertical total 100%) whose **adult attendance** 1985-1989:									
Grew %	28	31	32	31	36	35	(42)	27	33
Remained static %	67	63	66	64	60	62	(50)	64	63
Declined %	5	6	2	5	4	3	(8)	9	4

[1] Figures sum to more than 100% because multiple answers were possible

Age and sex of churchgoers 1979 and 1989

Age-Group	Population 1979			Churchgoers in 1979			Churchgoers in 1989[1]			Population 1989		
	Men %	Women %	Total %	Men %	Women %	Total %	Men %	Women %	Total %	Men %	Women %	Total %
Under 15	11	10	21	16	15	31	16	15	31	10	9	19
15-19	4	4	8	4	5	9	9	7	16	4	4	8
20-29	7	7	14	7	6	13	7	6	13	8	8	16
30-44	10	9	19	8	9	17	8	10	18	10	10	20
45-64	11	12	23	6	8	14	6	7	13	11	11	22
65 and over	6	9	15	6	10	16	3	6	9	6	9	15
All ages	49	51	100	47	53	100	49	51	100	49	51	100

[1] This table is based on responses from 45% of all Independent churches in England

Church environment

Percentage of all churches 1989 %	City Centre 4	Inner City 8	Council Estate 8	Suburban/ Urban Fringe 30	Separate Town 18	Other built-up area 6	Rural area: Commuter dormitory 11	Rural area: Other 15	ALL Churches 100
Children attending:									
1985	3,000	5,500	5,500	44,000	20,100	6,500	19,700	14,300	118,600
⇩ 4 years	+13%	+9%	+67%	+5%	+15%	+2%	+16%	+8%	+12%
1989	3,400	6,000	9,200	46,000	23,200	6,600	22,900	15,400	132,700
Percentage of total ⇨ %	2	5	7	35	17	5	17	12	100
Adults attending:									
1985	10,200	29,400	11,900	88,500	58,300	14,700	29,600	14,900	257,500
⇩ 4 years	+24%	−1%	+18%	+21%	+6%	+13%	+17%	+14%	+14%
1989	12,600	29,000	14,100	107,300	61,500	16,600	34,700	17,000	292,800
Percentage of total ⇨ %	4	10	5	37	21	6	12	6	100
Membership:									
1985	9,500	28,600	16,100	44,500	35,200	12,200	33,900	18,600	198,600
⇩ 4 years	+9%	+6%	+9%	+39%	+24%	+16%	−8%	−31%	+12%
1989	10,400	30,400	17,500	61,900	43,700	14,100	31,300	12,800	222,100
Percentage of total ⇨ %	5	14	8	28	19	6	14	6	100
Percentage ⇩ of churches in each category (vertical total 100%) whose **adult attendance** 1985-1989:									
Grew %	35	39	29	36	38	28	26	17	33
Remained static %	57	58	65	59	57	67	73	81	63
Declined %	8	3	6	5	5	5	1	2	4
Percentage ⇩ of churches in each category (vertical total 100%) in 1985 whose **services** were held:									
Morning only %	21	11	10	34	32	42	32	25	35
Morning & Evening %	46	55	74	59	61	44	47	51	59
Evening only %	33	34	16	7	7	14	21	24	16
Percentage ⇩ of churches in each category (vertical total 100%) in 1989 whose **services** were held:									
Morning only %	25	17	11	32	38	32	42	29	32
Morning & Evening %	57	60	73	64	59	59	58	49	58
Evening only %	18	23	16	4	3	9	10	22	10

Size[1] of church by weekly adult attendance 1979 and 1989[2]

	10 or under	11-25	26-50	51-100	101-150	151-200	201-300	301-400	401-500	Over 500	Average size[1]	Number (=100%)
ALL Churches 1979 %	6	30	23	23	5	5	4	3	1	—	60	3,430
ALL Churches 1989 %	5	24	22	18	9	6	7	4	2	3	93	4,123
Growing churches[3] %	0	14	20	24	14	6	10	5	2	5	121	1,362
Static churches[3] %	10	28	24	12	6	6	5	4	2	3	83	2,589
Declining churches[3] %	15	20	8	41	6	4	3	1	2	—	59	172

[1] Total of morning and evening services (when both held) with those attending both times counted twice
[2] This table is based on responses from 51% of all Independent churches in 1989   [3] 1989 figures

AFRO-CARIBBEAN

1989 Afro-Caribbean adult church attendance as percentage of adult population:	0.2%
1989 Afro-Caribbean adult church attendance as percentage of all adult church attendance:	2%
1989 Afro-Caribbean child church attendance as percentage of child population:	0.4%
1989 Afro-Caribbean child church attendance as percentage of all child church attendance:	3%
Percentage of churches responding:	47%

Churchmanship of church and people

Percentage of all churches 1989 ⇨ %	Broad Evan-gelical	Main-stream Evan-gelical	Charis-matic Evan-gelical	Total Evan-gelical	Low Church	Broad	Liberal	Anglo-Catholic	Catholic	All Others	ALL Churches
	4	20	67	91	1	1	2	0	1	4	100
Children attending:											
1985	1,300	9,000	26,000	36,300	400	100	400	100	100	800	38,200
⇩ 4 years	−8%	−9%	−6%	−7%	−25%	+100%	0%	0%	0%	−13%	−7%
1989	1,200	8,200	24,400	33,800	300	200	400	100	100	700	35,600
Percentage of total ⇨ %	3	23	69	95	1	1	1	0	0	2	100
Adults attending:											
1985	2,400	12,200	43,300	57,900	400	300	1,200	100	6,300	1,300	67,500
⇩ 4 years	+13%	−14%	+7%	+3%	−25%	0%	−8%	0%	−8%	+8%	+1%
1989	2,700	10,500	46,300	59,500	300	300	1,100	100	5,800	1,400	68,500
Percentage of total ⇨ %	4	15	68	87	½	½	2	0	8	2	100
Membership:											
1985	1,600	24,400	25,700	51,700	200	2,200	700	★	9,600	1,000	65,400
⇩ 4 years	−6%	+15%	+7%	+10%	−50%	−45%	−14%	−	−19%	+30%	+4%
1989	1,500	28,000	27,600	57,100	100	1,200	600	100	7,800	1,300	68,200
Percentage of total ⇨ %	2	41	41	84	0	2	1	0	11	2	100
Percentage ⇩ of churches in each category (vertical total 100%) whose **adult attendance** 1985-1989:											
Grew %	(31)	25	30	30	(0)	(0)	(0)	−	(0)	37	29
Remained static %	(69)	55	63	63	(100)	(100)	(100)	−	(100)	41	64
Declined %	(0)	20	7	7	(0)	(0)	(0)	−	(0)	22	7

Year church/congregation founded

	Before 1500	1500-1799	1800-1849	1850-1874	1875-1899	1900-1924	1925-1949	1950-1974	1975 or later	ALL Churches
Percentage of all churches **1989** ⇨ %	0	0	0	0	0	0	0	57	43	100
Percentage ⇩ of churches in each category (vertical total 100%) whose **adult attendance** 1985-1989:										
Grew %	−	−	−	−	−	−	−	26	32	29
Remained static %	−	−	−	−	−	−	−	68	61	64
Declined %	−	−	−	−	−	−	−	6	7	7

Types of Third World Community Aid church would support

Percentage of all churches **1989** ⇨ %	Project activities	Specific Geographical area	Named communities	Named individuals	Administered through local churches	Evangelism/ missionary work	Other	No support	TOTAL ALL Churches
	13	17	4	16	31	84	1	2	168[1]
Percentage ⇩ of churches in each category (vertical total 100%) whose **adult attendance** 1985-1989:									
Grew %	36	29	(8)	42	26	28	†	†	29
Remained static %	57	65	(83)	47	68	66	†	†	64
Declined %	7	6	(9)	11	6	6	†	†	7

[1] Figures sum to more than 100% because multiple answers were possible

Age and sex of churchgoers 1979 and 1989

Age-Group	Population 1979			Churchgoers in 1979			Churchgoers in 1989[1]			Population 1989		
	Men %	Women %	Total %	Men %	Women %	Total %	Men %	Women %	Total %	Men %	Women %	Total %
Under 15	11	10	21	19	19	38	15	19	34	10	9	19
15-19	4	4	8	4	8	12	4	5	9	4	4	8
20-29	7	7	14	4	6	10	6	11	17	8	8	16
30-44	10	9	19	7	11	18	7	9	16	10	10	20
45-64	11	12	23	6	11	17	7	11	18	11	11	22
65 and over	6	9	15	1	4	5	2	4	6	6	9	15
All ages	49	51	100	41	59	100	41	59	100	49	51	100

[1] This table is based on responses from 25% of all Afro-Caribbean churches in England

Church environment

	City Centre	Inner City	Council Estate	Suburban/ Urban Fringe	Separate Town	Other built-up area	Rural area: Commuter dormitory	Rural area: Other	ALL Churches
Percentage of all churches 1989 %	7	50	14	14	7	6	1	1	100
Children attending:									
1985	1,700	20,000	6,100	4,000	3,400	2,400	500	100	38,200
⇩ 4 years	+6%	0%	−36%	+18%	−35%	0%	+20%	0%	−7%
1989	1,800	19,900	3,900	4,700	2,200	2,400	600	100	35,600
Percentage of total ⇨ %	5	56	11	13	6	7	2	0	100
Adults attending:									
1985	3,300	43,600	7,900	4,500	4,000	3,200	800	200	67,500
⇩ 4 years	+3%	−8%	+23%	+53%	−15%	+9%	+50%	+50%	+1%
1989	3,400	40,100	9,700	6,900	3,400	3,500	1,200	300	68,500
Percentage of total ⇨ %	5	59	14	10	5	5	2	0	100
Membership:									
1985	2,000	35,100	10,900	11,600	2,700	2,000	900	200	65,400
⇩ 4 years	+35%	+9%	−7%	−4%	+7%	+15%	−11%	0%	+4%
1989	2,700	38,100	10,100	11,100	2,900	2,300	800	200	68,200
Percentage of total ⇨ %	4	56	15	16	4	3	1	0	100
Percentage ⇩ of churches in each category (vertical total 100%) whose **adult attendance** 1985-1989:									
Grew %	40	33	33	13	13	13	†	†	16
Remained static %	40	61	60	81	87	87	†	†	73
Declined %	20	6	7	6	0	0	†	†	11
Percentage ⇩ of churches in each category (vertical total 100%) in 1985 whose **services** were held:									
Morning only %	0	6	0	23	0	†	†	†	9
Morning & Evening %	42	87	100	77	100	†	†	†	84
Evening only %	58	7	0	0	0	†	†	†	7
Percentage ⇩ of churches in each category (vertical total 100%) in 1989 whose **services** were held:									
Morning only %	0	12	0	21	0	†	†	†	10
Morning & Evening %	61	83	100	79	100	†	†	†	84
Evening only %	39	5	0	0	0	†	†	†	6

Size[1] of church by weekly adult attendance 1979 and 1989[2]

	10 or under	11-25	26-50	51-100	101-150	151-200	201-300	301-400	401-500	Over 500	Average size[1]	Number (=100%)
ALL Churches 1979 %	4	14	26	23	14	11	4	2	2	—	80	822
ALL Churches 1989 %	5	17	22	14	15	10	9	4	2	2	102	949
Growing churches[3] %	0	13	10	15	26	22	15	4	1	—	128	275
Static churches[3] %	5	17	27	13	5	5	8	4	3	4	97	608
Declining churches[3] %	13	34	20	20	13	—	—	—	—	—	36	66

[1] Total of morning and evening services (when both held) with those attending both times counted twice
[2] This table is based on responses from 29% of all Afro-Caribbean churches in 1989   [3] 1989 figures

PENTECOSTALS

1989 Pentecostal adult church attendance
as percentage of adult population: 0.2%

1989 Pentecostal adult church attendance
as percentage of all adult church attendance: 3%

1989 Pentecostal child church attendance
as percentage of child population: 0.4%

1989 Pentecostal child church attendance
as percentage of all child church attendance: 3%

Percentage of churches responding: 57%

Churchmanship of church and people

Percentage of all churches	Broad Evan-gelical	Main-stream Evan-gelical	Charis-matic Evan-gelical	Total Evan-gelical	Low Church	Broad	Liberal	Anglo-Catholic	Catholic	All Others	ALL Churches
1989 ⇨ %	1	11	83	95	1	1	0	0	0	3	100
Children attending:											
1985	300	3,500	30,700	34,500	100	100	★	0	300	400	35,400
⇩ 4 years	−33%	+26%	+3%	+5%	+100%	0%	−	−	−33%	+25%	+6%
1989	200	4,400	31,700	36,300	200	100	100	0	200	500	37,400
Percentage of total ⇨ %	1	12	84	97	1	0	0	0	1	1	100
Adults attending:											
1985	500	7,400	74,600	82,500	200	200	★	0	700	1,300	84,900
⇩ 4 years	+20%	0%	+12%	+11%	+200%	+100%	−	−	−71%	+92%	+11%
1989	600	7,400	83,300	91,300	600	400	200	0	200	2,500	95,200
Percentage of total ⇨ %	1	8	87	96	1	0	0	0	0	3	100
Membership:											
1985	400	5,500	52,000	57,900	400	200	★	0	100	1,500	60,100
⇩ 4 years	0%	−9%	+13%	+11%	+25%	+100%	−	−	0%	+80%	+13%
1989	400	5,000	58,700	64,100	500	400	200	0	100	2,700	68,000
Percentage of total ⇨ %	1	7	86	94	1	1	0	0	0	4	100

Percentage ⇩ of churches in each category (vertical total 100%) whose **adult attendance** 1985-1989:

		Broad Evan-gelical	Main-stream Evan-gelical	Charis-matic Evan-gelical	Total Evan-gelical	Low Church	Broad	Liberal	Anglo-Catholic	Catholic	All Others	ALL Churches
Grew	%	(6)	7	38	34	(67)	(51)	−	−	−	(62)	35
Remained static	%	(91)	78	56	59	(33)	(49)	−	−	−	(25)	58
Declined	%	(3)	15	6	7	(0)	(0)	−	−	−	(13)	7

Year church/congregation founded

		Before 1500	1500-1799	1800-1849	1850-1874	1875-1899	1900-1924	1925-1949	1950-1974	1975 or later	ALL Churches
Percentage of all churches 1989 ⇨ %		0	0	0	0	0	7	43	25	25	100

Percentage ⇩ of churches in each category (vertical total 100%) whose **adult attendance** 1985-1989:

		Before 1500	1500-1799	1800-1849	1850-1874	1875-1899	1900-1924	1925-1949	1950-1974	1975 or later	ALL Churches
Grew	%	−	−	−	−	−	30	34	33	43	35
Remained static	%	−	−	−	−	−	63	59	58	52	58
Declined	%	−	−	−	−	−	7	7	9	5	7

Types of Third World Community Aid church would support

Percentage of all churches 1989 ⇨ %		Project activities	Specific Geographical area	Named communities	Named individuals	Administered through local churches	Evangelism/ missionary work	Other	No support	TOTAL ALL Churches
		13	20	4	21	33	89	1	2	183[1]

Percentage ⇩ of churches in each category (vertical total 100%) whose **adult attendance** 1985-1989:

		Project activities	Specific Geographical area	Named communities	Named individuals	Administered through local churches	Evangelism/ missionary work	Other	No support	TOTAL ALL Churches
Grew	%	27	38	(54)	40	38	35	†	(38)	35
Remained static	%	65	53	(46)	59	55	59	†	(46)	58
Declined	%	8	9	(0)	1	7	6	†	(16)	7

[1] Figures sum to more than *100%* because multiple answers were possible

Age and sex of churchgoers 1979 and 1989

Age-Group	Population 1979			Churchgoers in 1979			Churchgoers in 1989[1]			Population 1989		
	Men %	Women %	Total %	Men %	Women %	Total %	Men %	Women %	Total %	Men %	Women %	Total %
Under 15	11	10	21	15	14	29	13	15	28	10	9	19
15-19	4	4	8	5	6	11	4	5	9	4	4	8
20-29	7	7	14	6	7	13	6	7	13	8	8	16
30-44	10	9	19	8	9	17	9	11	20	10	10	20
45-64	11	12	23	7	9	16	7	10	17	11	11	22
65 and over	6	9	15	5	9	14	5	8	13	6	9	15
All ages	49	51	100	46	54	100	44	56	100	49	51	100

[1] This table is based on responses from 51% of all Pentecostal churches in England

Church environment

Percentage of all churches 1989 %	City Centre 3	Inner City 13	Council Estate 13	Suburban/ Urban Fringe 25	Separate Town 25	Other built-up area 7	Rural area: Commuter dormitory 6	Rural area: Other 8	ALL Churches 100
Children attending:									
1985	2,600	3,600	4,000	11,800	7,000	2,800	1,800	1,800	35,400
⇩ 4 years	+8%	+3%	−5%	+13%	+1%	0%	0%	+17%	+6%
1989	2,800	3,700	3,800	13,300	7,100	2,800	1,800	2,100	37,400
Percentage of total ⇨ %	7	10	10	36	19	7	5	6	100
Adults attending:									
1985	12,400	11,400	8,000	23,300	17,900	5,600	3,500	2,800	84,900
⇩ 4 years	−6%	+22%	+18%	+9%	+13%	+25%	+14%	+29%	+11%
1989	11,700	13,900	9,400	25,300	20,300	7,000	4,000	3,600	95,200
Percentage of total ⇨ %	12	15	10	27	21	7	4	4	100
Membership:									
1985	5,100	10,900	5,700	16,900	12,300	4,100	2,500	2,600	60,100
⇩ 4 years	−6%	+26%	+18%	+5%	+23%	+12%	+4%	+8%	+13%
1989	4,800	13,700	6,700	17,700	15,100	4,600	2,600	2,800	68,000
Percentage of total ⇨ %	7	20	10	26	22	7	4	4	100
Percentage ⇩ of churches in each category (vertical total 100%) whose **adult attendance** 1985-1989:									
Grew %	33	44	30	33	37	35	46	20	35
Remained static %	50	48	64	60	61	53	46	67	58
Declined %	17	8	6	7	2	12	8	13	7
Percentage ⇩ of churches in each category (vertical total 100%) in 1985 whose **services** were held:									
Morning only %	†	7	5	7	3	8	10	8	6
Morning & Evening %	†	87	91	91	93	85	82	66	88
Evening only %	†	6	4	2	4	7	8	26	6
Percentage ⇩ of churches in each category (vertical total 100%) in 1989 whose **services** were held:									
Morning only %	(9)	8	6	7	4	10	12	9	7
Morning & Evening %	(82)	86	91	91	94	82	79	60	87
Evening only %	(9)	6	3	2	2	8	9	31	6

Size[1] of church by weekly adult attendance 1979 and 1989[2]

	10 or under	11-25	26-50	51-100	101-150	151-200	201-300	301-400	401-500	Over 500	Average size[1]	Number (=100%)
ALL Churches 1979 %	1	16	25	16	15	14	9	2	2	—	93	950
ALL Churches 1989 %	2	5	12	22	16	20	12	4	4	3	141	1,002
Growing churches[3] %	0	9	10	20	22	21	15	4	4	4	160	351
Static churches[3] %	2	4	14	18	16	24	12	4	4	2	140	581
Declining churches[3] %	19	11	3	50	11	6	—	—	—	—	52	70

[1] Total of morning and evening services (when both held) with those attending both times counted twice
[2] This table is based on responses from 56% of all Pentecostal churches in 1989   [3] 1989 figures

OTHER FREE CHURCHES

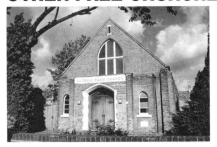

1989 Other Free Churches adult church attendance
as percentage of adult population: **0.2%**

1989 Other Free Churches adult church attendance
as percentage of all adult church attendance: **2%**

1989 Other Free Churches child church attendance
as percentage of child population: **0.4%**

1989 Other Free Churches child church attendance
as percentage of all child church attendance: **2%**

Percentage of churches responding: **65%**

Churchmanship of church and people

Percentage of all churches	Broad Evan-gelical	Main-stream Evan-gelical	Charis-matic Evan-gelical	Total Evan-gelical	Low Church	Broad	Liberal	Anglo-Catholic	Catholic	All Others	ALL Churches
1989 ⇨ %	*21*	*43*	*4*	*69*	*6*	*8*	*13*	*0*	*0*	*4*	*100*
Children attending:											
1985	11,200	18,000	1,700	30,900	1,500	700	1,600	0	★	200	34,900
⇩ 4 years	−14%	−11%	−6%	−12%	−13%	−14%	−31%	−	−	+50%	−12%
1989	9,600	16,000	1,600	27,200	1,300	600	1,100	0	100	300	30,600
Percentage of total ⇨ %	32	52	5	89	4	2	4	0	0	1	100
Adults attending:											
1985	24,600	40,600	3,200	68,400	4,100	2,800	4,600	★	200	1,300	81,400
⇩ 4 years	−2%	−1%	+3%	−1%	+17%	+36%	+9%	−	+50%	+23%	+2%
1989	24,000	40,200	3,300	67,500	4,800	3,800	5,000	★	300	1,600	83,000
Percentage of total ⇨ %	29	48	4	81	6	5	6	0	0	2	100
Membership:											
1985	29,200	45,400	3,800	78,400	5,200	6,200	8,900	★	300	2,600	101,600
⇩ 4 years	+21%	−11%	−8%	+1%	+8%	0%	−1%	−	0%	+15%	+2%
1989	35,300	40,500	3,500	79,300	5,600	6,200	8,800	★	300	3,000	103,200
Percentage of total ⇨ %	34	39	4	77	5	6	9	0	0	3	100

Percentage ⇩ of churches in each category (vertical total 100%) whose **adult attendance** 1985-1989:

Grew %	19	15	26	18	19	53	5	−	−	0	18
Remained static %	77	70	56	73	76	37	85	−	−	79	73
Declined %	4	15	18	9	5	10	10	−	−	21	9

Year church/congregation founded

	Before 1500	1500-1799	1800-1849	1850-1874	1875-1899	1900-1924	1925-1949	1950-1974	1975 or later	ALL Churches
Percentage of all churches 1989 ⇨ %	*0*	*16*	*3*	*4*	*39*	*9*	*12*	*11*	*6*	*100*

Percentage ⇩ of churches in each category (vertical total 100%) whose **adult attendance** 1985-1989:

	Before 1500	1500-1799	1800-1849	1850-1874	1875-1899	1900-1924	1925-1949	1950-1974	1975 or later	ALL Churches
Grew %	−	└── 10 ──┘		18	20	11	9	23	19	18
Remained static %	−	87		70	68	86	86	74	75	73
Declined %	−	3		12	12	3	5	3	6	9

Types of Third World Community Aid church would support

Percentage of all churches 1989 ⇨ %	Project activities	Specific Geographical area	Named communities	Named individuals	Administered through local churches	Evangelism/ missionary work	Other	No support	TOTAL ALL Churches[1]
	47	*23*	*14*	*16*	*26*	*53*	*2*	*1*	*182*[1]

Percentage ⇩ of churches in each category (vertical total 100%) whose **adult attendance** 1985-1989:

	Project activities	Specific Geographical area	Named communities	Named individuals	Administered through local churches	Evangelism/ missionary work	Other	No support	TOTAL ALL Churches
Grew %	19	27	8	19	14	20	(0)	†	18
Remained static %	73	63	79	69	80	72	(82)	†	73
Declined %	8	10	13	12	6	8	(18)	†	9

[1] Figures sum to more than *100%* because multiple answers were possible

OTHER FREE CHURCHES

Age and sex of churchgoers 1979 and 1989

Age-Group	Population 1979			Churchgoers in 1979			Churchgoers in 1989[1]			Population 1989		
	Men %	Women %	Total %	Men %	Women %	Total %	Men %	Women %	Total %	Men %	Women %	Total %
Under 15	11	10	21	11	14	25	12	15	27	10	9	19
15-19	4	4	8	4	5	9	2	4	6	4	4	8
20-29	7	7	14	5	6	11	4	4	8	8	8	16
30-44	10	9	19	7	9	16	6	8	14	10	10	20
45-64	11	12	23	9	11	20	9	12	21	11	11	22
65 and over	6	9	15	8	11	19	8	16	24	6	9	15
All ages	49	51	100	44	56	100	41	59	100	49	51	100

[1] This table is based on responses from 57% of all Other Free churches in England

Church environment

Percentage of all churches 1989 %	City Centre	Inner City	Council Estate	Suburban/ Urban Fringe	Separate Town	Other built-up area	Rural area: Commuter dormitory	Rural area: Other	ALL Churches
	3	10	9	29	24	5	7	13	100
Children attending:									
1985	900	2,200	3,800	10,400	11,000	2,000	2,400	2,200	34,900
4 years	−22%	−18%	−34%	−6%	−13%	0%	−21%	+5%	−12%
1989	700	1,800	2,500	9,800	9,600	2,000	1,900	2,300	30,600
Percentage of total %	2	6	8	32	31	7	6	8	100
Adults attending:									
1985	2,600	9,700	4,700	27,700	20,600	5,300	4,600	6,200	81,400
4 years	+4%	−1%	−2%	−1%	+12%	−8%	−11%	+8%	+2%
1989	2,700	9,600	4,600	27,300	23,100	4,900	4,100	6,700	83,000
Percentage of total %	3	12	5	33	28	6	5	8	100
Membership:									
1985	3,000	11,300	5,600	37,200	24,900	6,000	6,800	6,800	101,600
4 years	+10%	+11%	−7%	+4%	−1%	0%	−16%	+3%	+2%
1989	3,300	12,500	5,200	38,800	24,700	6,000	5,700	7,000	103,200
Percentage of total %	3	12	5	37	24	6	6	7	100
Percentage of churches in each category (vertical total 100%) whose **adult attendance** 1985-1989:									
Grew %	8	24	13	19	21	17	15	14	18
Remained static %	84	71	83	64	72	75	74	86	73
Declined %	8	5	4	17	7	8	11	0	9
Percentage of churches in each category (vertical total 100%) in 1985 whose **services** were held:									
Morning only %	13	31	7	25	17	20	24	46	24
Morning & Evening %	27	51	59	59	68	57	49	39	55
Evening only %	60	18	34	16	15	23	27	15	21
Percentage of churches in each category (vertical total 100%) in 1989 whose **services** were held:									
Morning only %	22	48	33	40	27	16	34	53	36
Morning & Evening %	37	45	23	53	65	69	50	39	52
Evening only %	41	7	44	7	8	15	16	8	12

Size[1] of church by weekly adult attendance 1979 and 1989[2]

	10 or under	11-25	26-50	51-100	101-150	151-200	201-300	301-400	401-500	Over 500	Average size[1]	Number (=100%)
ALL Churches 1979 %	8	14	19	29	11	8	6	3	2	—	81	1,456
ALL Churches 1989 %	3	24	27	18	9	7	7	3	1	1	78	1,462
Growing churches[3] %	0	15	21	23	15	10	7	4	3	2	107	263
Static churches[3] %	2	29	31	14	5	7	7	3	1	1	73	1,067
Declining churches[3] %	24	10	5	39	13	3	3	3	—	—	60	132

[1] Total of morning and evening services (when both held) with those attending both times counted twice
[2] This table is based on responses from 68% of all Other Free churches in 1989   [3] 1989 figures

TOTAL FREE CHURCHES

1989 Free Church adult church attendance as percentage of adult population:	3.2%
1989 Free Church adult church attendance as percentage of all adult church attendance:	34%
1989 Free Church child church attendance as percentage of child population:	5.2%
1989 Free Church child church attendance as percentage of all child church attendance:	38%
Percentage of churches responding:	72%

Churchmanship of church and people

Percentage of all churches 1989 ⇨ %	Broad Evan-gelical	Main-stream Evan-gelical	Charis-matic Evan-gelical	Total Evan-gelical	Low Church	Broad	Liberal	Anglo-Catholic	Catholic	All Others	ALL Churches
	16	21	19	56	13	13	13	1	1	3	100
Children attending:											
1985	66,500	128,100	140,100	334,700	41,100	46,800	52,800	2,000	2,200	6,500	486,100
⇩ 4 years	−14%	−8%	+6%	−3%	−14%	−9%	−14%	+75%	+18%	+3%	−6%
1989	57,000	117,700	148,600	323,300	35,200	42,500	45,500	3,500	2,600	6,700	459,300
Percentage of total ⇨ %	12	26	32	70	8	9	10	1	½	1½	100
Adults attending:											
1985	206,000	219,300	279,000	704,300	112,300	170,400	185,700	15,600	22,300	19,100	1,229,700
⇩ 4 years	−6%	+1%	+13%	+4%	+2%	−7%	−4%	+16%	+26%	+20%	+2%
1989	193,800	220,800	314,500	729,100	115,100	158,100	177,500	18,100	28,100	23,000	1,249,000
Percentage of total ⇨ %	16	18	25	59	9	13	14	1	2	2	100
Membership:											
1985	196,600	232,200	218,300	647,100	117,400	156,800	170,300	12,700	28,700	22,500	1,155,500
⇩ 4 years	+4%	0%	+14%	+6%	−3%	−8%	−3%	−31%	−1%	+14%	+2%
1989	205,100	232,600	249,300	687,000	113,500	145,000	165,700	8,800	28,500	25,700	1,174,200
Percentage of total ⇨ %	18	20	21	59	10	12	14	1	2	2	100

Percentage ⇩ of churches in each category (vertical total 100%) whose **adult attendance** 1985-1989:

Grew %	21	24	40	27	14	18	16	(39)	24	16	24
Remained static %	75	64	53	66	77	70	74	(61)	59	73	68
Declined %	4	12	7	7	9	12	10	(0)	17	11	8

Year church/congregation founded

	Before 1500	1500-1799	1800-1849	1850-1874	1875-1899	1900-1924	1925-1949	1950-1974	1975 or later	ALL Churches
Percentage of all churches 1989 ⇨ %	0	9	16	14	19	11	10	11	10	100
Percentage ⇩ of churches in each category (vertical total 100%) whose **adult attendance** 1985-1989:										
Grew %	—	25	23	18	22	21	25	28	45	24
Remained static %	—	69	69	75	69	70	68	62	49	68
Declined %	—	6	8	7	9	9	7	10	6	8

Types of Third World Community Aid church would support

Percentage of all churches 1989 ⇨ %	Project activities	Specific Geographical area	Named communities	Named individuals	Administered through local churches	Evangelism/ missionary work	Other	No support	TOTAL ALL Churches
	34	14	8	16	41	60	1	1	175[1]
Percentage ⇩ of churches in each category (vertical total 100%) whose **adult attendance** 1985-1989:									
Grew %	23	27	21	30	24	26	22	26	24
Remained static %	68	63	69	62	68	67	70	65	68
Declined %	9	10	10	8	8	7	8	9	8

[1] Figures sum to more than 100% because multiple answers were possible

Age and sex of churchgoers 1979 and 1989

Age-Group	Population 1979			Churchgoers in 1979			Churchgoers in 1989[1]			Population 1989		
	Men %	Women %	Total %	Men %	Women %	Total %	Men %	Women %	Total %	Men %	Women %	Total %
Under 15	11	10	21	15	15	30	12	15	27	10	9	19
15-19	4	4	8	3	4	7	4	4	8	4	4	8
20-29	7	7	14	4	5	9	5	5	10	8	8	16
30-44	10	9	19	7	8	15	7	9	16	10	10	20
45-64	11	12	23	7	12	19	7	12	19	11	11	22
65 and over	6	9	15	7	13	20	6	14	20	6	9	15
All ages	49	51	100	43	57	100	41	59	100	49	51	100

[1] This table is based on responses from 58% of all Free churches in England

Church environment

Percentage of all churches 1989 %	City Centre 3	Inner City 8	Council Estate 6	Suburban/ Urban Fringe 26	Separate Town 15	Other built-up area 5	Rural area: Commuter dormitory 12	Rural area: Other 25	ALL Churches 100
Children attending:									
1985	12,100	38,700	32,000	169,500	92,300	25,800	57,500	58,200	486,100
4 years	+3%	−4%	−9%	−4%	−3%	−6%	−5%	−16%	−6%
1989	12,500	37,300	29,200	163,000	89,900	24,200	54,500	48,700	459,300
Percentage of total %	3	8	6	35	20	5	12	11	100
Adults attending:									
1985	53,600	138,800	60,100	416,500	249,600	64,900	119,800	126,400	1,229,700
4 years	+5%	−3%	+9%	+2%	+1%	+8%	−1%	0%	+2%
1989	56,100	135,200	65,500	425,500	252,000	69,800	118,500	126,400	1,249,000
Percentage of total %	4	11	5	34	20	6	10	10	100
Membership:									
1985	44,500	126,100	65,300	376,600	229,500	62,400	123,600	127,500	1,155,500
4 years	+4%	+6%	+1%	+3%	+3%	+5%	−6%	−5%	+2%
1989	46,400	133,800	66,000	388,800	237,000	65,700	115,600	120,900	1,174,200
Percentage of total %	4	11	6	33	20	6	10	10	100
Percentage of churches in each category (vertical total 100%) whose **adult attendance** 1985-1989:									
Grew %	27	30	22	25	30	24	23	15	24
Remained static %	55	60	72	66	62	69	72	80	68
Declined %	18	10	6	9	8	7	5	5	8
Percentage of churches in each category (vertical total 100%) in 1985 whose **services** were held:									
Morning only %	23	15	18	20	18	33	24	29	23
Morning & Evening %	53	77	69	75	78	58	60	34	58
Evening only %	24	8	13	5	4	9	16	37	15
Percentage of churches in each category (vertical total 100%) in 1989 whose **services** were held:									
Morning only %	21	20	21	22	22	26	36	32	26
Morning & Evening %	61	66	65	74	74	67	53	33	60
Evening only %	18	14	14	4	4	7	11	35	14

Size[1] of church by weekly adult attendance 1979 and 1989[2]

	10 or under	11-25	26-50	51-100	101-150	151-200	201-300	301-400	401-500	Over 500	Average size[1]	Number (=100%)
ALL Churches 1979 %	5	22	24	22	12	6	6	2	1	—	69	18,334
ALL Churches 1989 %	2	7	25	28	20	10	4	2	1	1	87	18,296
Growing churches[3] %	0	2	7	28	32	17	8	3	2	1	123	4,467
Static churches[3] %	2	9	34	27	14	7	3	2	1	1	75	12,357
Declining churches[3] %	3	10	11	32	28	13	2	1	—	—	82	1,472

[1] Total of morning and evening services (when both held) with those attending both times counted twice
[2] This table is based on responses from 63% of all Free churches in 1989   [3] 1989 figures

ANGLICANS

1989 Anglican adult church attendance as percentage of adult population: 2.9%

1989 Anglican adult church attendance as percentage of all adult church attendance: 31%

1989 Anglican child church attendance as percentage of child population: 3.9%

1989 Anglican child church attendance as percentage of all child church attendance: 28%

Percentage of churches responding: 75%

Churchmanship of church and people

Percentage of all churches	Broad Evan-gelical	Main-stream Evan-gelical	Charis-matic Evan-gelical	Total Evan-gelical	Low Church	Broad	Liberal	Anglo-Catholic	Catholic	All Others	ALL Churches
1989 ⇨ %	9	2	7	18	13	23	18	12	14	2	100
Children attending:											
1985	51,400	13,500	53,500	118,400	32,700	61,200	66,700	37,300	48,100	2,900	367,300
⇩ 4 years	−4%	−21%	−5%	−7%	−1%	−4%	+1%	−9%	−12%	−7%	−5%
1989	49,200	10,600	50,900	110,200	32,500	58,700	67,100	33,800	42,500	2,700	348,000
Percentage of total ⇨ %	14	3	15	32	9	17	19	10	12	1	100
Adults attending:											
1985	143,100	34,300	113,300	290,700	130,800	217,500	231,300	149,500	140,900	20,300	1,181,000
⇩ 4 years	+2%	+15%	−6%	+1%	−9%	−4%	−3%	−7%	+2%	−14%	−3%
1989	146,500	39,500	106,200	292,200	118,400	209,400	223,300	139,400	143,800	17,400	1,143,900
Percentage of total ⇨ %	13	4	9	26	10	18	20	12	13	1	100
Membership:											
1985	219,300	44,300	167,000	430,600	191,900	339,300	345,100	174,700	162,500	31,200	1,675,300
⇩ 4 years	−8%	+10%	−7%	−6%	−3%	−3%	−7%	−9%	−16%	−42%	−7%
1989	201,200	48,700	155,800	405,700	186,600	330,000	322,200	159,400	136,900	18,200	1,559,000
Percentage of total ⇨ %	13	3	10	26	12	21	21	10	9	1	100
Percentage ⇩ of churches in each category (vertical total 100%) whose **adult attendance** 1985-1989:											
Grew %	32	27	39	35	24	25	30	24	26	12	28
Remained static %	64	58	54	58	67	68	64	69	67	81	65
Declined %	4	15	7	7	9	7	6	7	7	7	7

Year church/congregation founded

	Before 1500	1500-1799	1800-1849	1850-1874	1875-1899	1900-1924	1925-1949	1950-1974	1975 or later	ALL Churches
Percentage of all churches 1989 ⇨ %	53	4	9	10	9	5	4	5	1	100
Percentage ⇩ of churches in each category (vertical total 100%) whose **adult attendance** 1985-1989:										
Grew %	28	21	31	29	25	25	27	32	35	28
Remained static %	66	73	59	63	67	70	65	63	61	65
Declined %	6	6	10	8	8	5	8	5	4	7

Types of Third World Community Aid church would support

Percentage of all churches 1989 ⇨ %	Project activities	Specific Geographical area	Named communities	Named individuals	Administered through local churches	Evangelism/ missionary work	Other	No support	TOTAL ALL Churches
	43	22	13	18	37	47	1	4	185[1]
Percentage ⇩ of churches in each category (vertical total 100%) whose **adult attendance** 1985-1989:									
Grew %	30	28	32	30	29	30	21	14	28
Remained static %	64	64	62	64	65	63	73	76	65
Declined %	6	8	6	6	6	7	6	10	7

[1] Figures sum to more than 100% because multiple answers were possible

Age and sex of churchgoers 1979 and 1989

Age-Group	Population 1979			Churchgoers in 1979			Churchgoers in 1989[1]			Population 1989		
	Men %	Women %	Total %	Men %	Women %	Total %	Men %	Women %	Total %	Men %	Women %	Total %
Under 15	11	10	21	14	13	27	13	13	26	10	9	19
15-19	4	4	8	4	5	9	2	3	5	4	4	8
20-29	7	7	14	4	6	10	3	5	8	8	8	16
30-44	10	9	19	7	10	17	6	10	16	10	10	20
45-64	11	12	23	9	9	18	8	15	23	11	11	22
65 and over	6	9	15	7	12	19	7	15	22	6	9	15
All ages	49	51	100	45	55	100	39	61	100	49	51	100

[1] This table is based on responses from 61% of all Anglican churches in England

Church environment

Percentage of all churches 1989 %	City Centre 6	Inner City 6	Council Estate 5	Suburban/ Urban Fringe 18	Separate Town 7	Other built-up area 3	Rural area: Commuter dormitory 20	Rural area: Other 35	ALL Churches 100
Children attending:									
1985	24,900	18,200	13,800	103,400	49,300	18,800	84,600	54,300	367,300
⇩ 4 years	−16%	−5%	−2%	−6%	−9%	0%	−4%	0%	−5%
1989	21,000	17,300	13,500	97,300	44,700	18,800	81,100	54,300	348,000
Percentage of total ⇨ %	6	5	4	28	13	5	23	16	100
Adults attending:									
1985	97,900	84,800	61,700	362,000	148,500	41,200	194,700	190,200	1,181,000
⇩ 4 years	−10%	−2%	−6%	−4%	−10%	+8%	0%	+1%	−3%
1989	88,400	83,000	58,200	348,300	133,800	44,500	195,200	192,500	1,143,900
Percentage of total ⇨ %	8	7	5	30	12	4	17	17	100
Membership:									
1985	103,100	93,700	77,700	469,100	232,300	69,800	322,700	306,900	1,675,300
⇩ 4 years	−15%	−17%	−25%	−8%	−3%	−7%	+1%	−6%	−7%
1989	87,800	78,100	58,300	430,600	224,600	65,000	324,900	289,700	1,559,000
Percentage of total ⇨ %	6	5	4	28	14	4	21	18	100
Percentage ⇩ of churches in each category (vertical total 100%) whose **adult attendance** 1985-1989:									
Grew %	27	24	33	29	35	31	30	21	28
Remained static %	66	67	59	64	59	60	64	73	65
Declined %	7	9	9	7	6	9	6	6	7
Percentage ⇩ of churches in each category (vertical total 100%) in 1985 whose **services** were held:									
Morning only %	18	31	39	20	16	20	40	51	39
Morning & Evening %	69	63	55	79	82	75	48	26	53
Evening only %	13	6	6	1	2	5	12	23	13
Percentage ⇩ of churches in each category (vertical total 100%) in 1989 whose **services** were held:									
Morning only %	27	37	46	24	25	30	55	66	49
Morning & Evening %	69	62	52	76	74	68	39	20	44
Evening only %	4	1	2	0	1	2	6	14	7

Size[1] of church by weekly adult attendance 1979 and 1989[2]

	10 or under	11-25	26-50	51-100	101-150	151-200	201-300	301-400	401-500	Over 500	Average size[1]	Number (=100%)
ALL Churches 1979 %	5	16	23	25	14	10	5	1	1/2	1/2	74	16,960
ALL Churches 1989 %	4	15	24	22	16	11	6	1½	—1/2—		77	16,373
Growing churches[3] %	0	3	14	24	26	19	9	3	1	1	117	4,582
Static churches[3] %	6	18	29	22	12	7	5	1	—	—	62	10,642
Declining churches[3] %	8	19	22	29	15	6	1	—	—	—	54	1,149

[1] Total of morning and evening services (when both held) with those attending both times counted twice
[2] This table is based on responses from 70% of all Anglican churches in 1989   [3] 1989 figures

ROMAN CATHOLICS

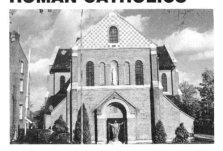

1989 Catholic adult church attendance as percentage of adult population: **3.4%**

1989 Catholic adult church attendance as percentage of all adult church attendance: **35%**

1989 Catholic child church attendance as percentage of child population: **4.6%**

1989 Catholic child church attendance as percentage of all child church attendance: **34%**

Percentage of churches responding: **51%**

Churchmanship of church and people

Percentage of all churches	Broad Evan-gelical	Main-stream Evan-gelical	Charis-matic Evan-gelical	Total Evan-gelical	Low Church	Broad	Liberal	Anglo-Catholic	Catholic	All Others	ALL Churches
1989 ⇨ %	0	0	1	1	0	0	1	0	97	1	100

Children attending:

1985	0	300	600	900	200	900	600	1,100	419,800	1,200	424,700
⇩ 4 years	—	+33%	−33%	−11%	0%	+11%	+50%	+18%	−3%	+17%	−3%
1989	0	400	400	800	200	1,000	900	1,300	405,700	1,400	411,300
Percentage of total ⇨ %	0	0	0	0	0	0	0	½	99	½	100

Adults attending:

1985	★	2,900	2,500	5,400	400	1,600	9,500	4,400	1,303,100	11,500	1,335,900
⇩ 4 years	—	−14%	+36%	+9%	−50%	+25%	−4%	−11%	−2%	−2%	−2%
1989	★	2,500	3,400	5,900	200	2,000	9,100	3,900	1,272,200	11,300	1,304,600
Percentage of total ⇨ %	0	0	0	0	0	0	1	0	98	1	100

Membership:

1985	100	7,100	13,100	20,300	500	12,200	39,900	43,200	3,861,200	29,200	4,006,500
⇩ 4 years	0%	−4%	+17%	+9%	0%	+24%	+23%	+18%	+4%	+14%	+5%
1989	100	6,800	15,300	22,200	500	15,100	49,000	50,900	4,026,200	33,200	4,197,100
Percentage of total ⇨ %	0	0	½	½	0	½	1	1	96	1	100

Percentage ⇩ of churches in each category (vertical total 100%) whose **adult attendance** 1985-1989:

Grew %	—	—	(68)	(68)	—	—	(42)	—	15	(52)	16
Remained static %	—	—	(32)	(32)	—	—	(58)	—	73	(48)	72
Declined %	—	—	(0)	(0)	—	—	(0)	—	12	(0)	12

Year church/congregation founded

	Before 1500	1500-1799	1800-1849	1850-1874	1875-1899	1900-1924	1925-1949	1950-1974	1975 or later	ALL Churches
Percentage of all churches 1989 ⇨ %	0	5	9	11	13	12	20	26	4	100

Percentage ⇩ of churches in each category (vertical total 100%) whose **adult attendance** 1985-1989:

Grew %	—	9	26	13	21	13	13	17	15	16
Remained static %	—	82	71	76	64	77	76	68	75	72
Declined %	—	9	3	11	15	10	11	15	10	12

Types of Third World Community Aid church would support

Percentage of all churches 1989 ⇨ %	Project activities	Specific Geographical area	Named communities	Named individuals	Administered through local churches	Evangelism/ missionary work	Other	No support	TOTAL ALL Churches
	62	22	23	10	34	32	1	0	184[1]

Percentage ⇩ of churches in each category (vertical total 100%) whose **adult attendance** 1985-1989:

Grew %	14	18	15	19	21	11	13	—	16
Remained static %	73	72	74	69	67	78	73	—	72
Declined %	13	10	11	12	12	11	14	—	12

[1] Figures sum to more than 100% because multiple answers were possible

Age and sex of churchgoers 1979 and 1989

Age-Group	Population 1979			Churchgoers in 1979			Churchgoers in 1989[1]			Population 1989		
	Men %	Women %	Total %	Men %	Women %	Total %	Men %	Women %	Total %	Men %	Women %	Total %
Under 15	11	10	21	12	12	24	12	12	24	10	9	19
15-19	4	4	8	5	7	12	3	5	8	4	4	8
20-29	7	7	14	5	7	12	4	7	11	8	8	16
30-44	10	9	19	9	10	19	8	10	18	10	10	20
45-64	11	12	23	9	11	20	11	12	23	11	11	22
65 and over	6	9	15	6	7	13	7	9	16	6	9	15
All ages	49	51	100	46	54	100	45	55	100	49	51	100

[1] This table is based on responses from 30% of all Roman Catholic churches in England

Church environment

	City Centre	Inner City	Council Estate	Suburban/ Urban Fringe	Separate Town	Other built-up area	Rural area: Commuter dormitory	Rural area: Other	ALL Churches
Percentage of all churches 1989 %	4	10	13	27	18	4	11	13	100
Children attending:									
1985	12,400	47,900	57,200	188,200	56,500	12,400	28,600	21,500	424,700
⇩ 4 years	+2%	+4%	0%	−6%	−4%	+18%	−4%	−9%	−3%
1989	12,600	49,700	57,000	176,400	54,000	14,600	27,400	19,600	411,300
Percentage of total ⇨ %	3	12	14	43	13	3	7	5	100
Adults attending:									
1985	59,100	157,000	178,800	511,200	181,000	64,100	89,400	95,300	1,335,900
⇩ 4 years	−7%	−4%	−3%	−3%	+12%	−17%	−3%	−6%	−2%
1989	54,900	150,900	173,800	493,900	202,100	53,400	86,400	89,200	1,304,600
Percentage of total ⇨ %	4	12	13	38	15	4	7	7	100
Membership:									
1985	214,600	467,000	532,400	1,605,200	625,100	138,300	238,900	185,000	4,006,500
⇩ 4 years	+5%	+1%	+5%	+6%	+6%	+8%	+3%	+4%	+5%
1989	224,400	471,600	559,000	1,695,700	660,300	149,400	244,900	191,800	4,197,100
Percentage of total ⇨ %	5	11	13	40	16	4	6	5	100
Percentage ⇩ of churches in each category (vertical total 100%) whose **adult attendance** 1985-1989:									
Grew %	17	16	14	15	13	7	16	21	16
Remained static %	72	72	75	71	80	86	68	69	72
Declined %	11	12	11	14	7	7	16	10	12
Percentage ⇩ of churches in each category (vertical total 100%) in 1985 whose **services** were held:									
Morning only %	21	45	40	20	24	36	45	58	35
Morning & Evening %	77	51	57	78	74	61	49	38	62
Evening only %	2	4	3	2	2	3	6	4	3
Percentage ⇩ of churches in each category (vertical total 100%) in 1989 whose **services** were held:									
Morning only %	21	47	47	24	31	34	47	52	39
Morning & Evening %	77	49	50	74	66	63	46	38	57
Evening only %	2	4	3	2	3	3	7	10	4

Size[1] of church by weekly adult attendance 1979 and 1989[2]

	10 or under	11-25	26-50	51-100	101-150	151-200	201-300	301-400	401-500	Over 500	Average size[1]	Number (=100%)
ALL Churches 1979 %	0	0	1	1	2	5	13	18	16	44	412	3,673
ALL Churches 1989 %	1	1	1	2	7	13	14	14	10	37	355	3,824
Growing churches[3] %	0	0	0	5	8	8	9	17	9	44	382	612
Static churches[3] %	1	1	1	2	7	11	16	12	11	38	360	2,791
Declining churches[3] %	0	0	6	0	9	19	21	21	8	16	282	421

[1] Total of morning and evening services (when both held) with those attending both times counted twice
[2] This table is based on responses from 48% of all Roman Catholic churches in 1989   [3] 1989 figures

ORTHODOX

1989 Orthodox adult church attendance as percentage of adult population: 0.0%

1989 Orthodox adult church attendance as percentage of all adult church attendance: 0.2%

1989 Orthodox child church attendance as percentage of child population: 0.0%

1989 Orthodox child church attendance as percentage of all child church attendance: 0.2%

Percentage of churches responding: 35%

Churchmanship of church and people

Percentage of all churches 1989 ⇨ %	Broad Evan-gelical	Main-stream Evan-gelical	Charis-matic Evan-gelical	Total Evan-gelical	Low Church	Broad	Liberal	Anglo-Catholic	Catholic	All Others	ALL Churches
	0	0	0	0	1	3	0	3	3	90	100
Children attending:											
1985	0	0	0	0	★	★	0	100	★	2,700	2,800
⇩ 4 years	–	–	–	–	–	–	–	0%	–	0%	+4%
1989	0	0	0	0	★	★	0	100	100	2,700	2,900
Percentage of total ⇨ %	0	0	0	0	0	0	0	3	3	94	100
Adults attending:											
1985	0	0	0	0	★	300	0	100	★	8,000	8,400
⇩ 4 years	–	–	–	–	–	+33%	–	0%	–	+10%	+12%
1989	0	0	0	0	★	400	0	100	100	8,800	9,400
Percentage of total ⇨ %	0	0	0	0	0	4	0	1	1	94	100
Membership:											
1985	0	0	0	0	★	3,200	0	200	1,900	214,700	220,000
⇩ 4 years	–	–	–	–	–	+3%	–	+50%	–11%	+6%	+6%
1989	0	0	0	0	200	3,300	0	300	1,700	226,600	232,100
Percentage of total ⇨ %	0	0	0	0	0	1	0	0	1	98	100

Percentage ⇩ of churches in each category (vertical total 100%) whose **adult attendance** 1985-1989:											
Grew %	–	–	–	–	†	(100)	–	(0)	†	30	33
Remained static %	–	–	–	–	†	(0)	–	(100)	†	70	67
Declined %	–	–	–	–	†	(0)	–	(0)	†	0	0

Year church/congregation founded

	Before 1500	1500-1799	1800-1849	1850-1874	1875-1899	1900-1924	1925-1949	1950-1974	1975 or later	ALL Churches
Percentage of all churches 1989 ⇨ %	0	0	0	0	0	0	13	55	32	100
Percentage ⇩ of churches in each category (vertical total 100%) whose **adult attendance** 1985-1989:										
Grew %	–	–	–	–	–	–	*Inadequate numbers*			33
Remained static %	–	–	–	–	–	–	*to give reliable*			67
Declined %	–	–	–	–	–	–	*percentages*			0

Types of Third World Community Aid church would support

Percentage of all churches 1989 ⇨ %	Project activities	Specific Geographical area	Named communities	Named individuals	Administered through local churches	Evangelism/ missionary work	Other	No support	TOTAL ALL Churches
	6	48	6	3	19	19	0	19	120[1]
Percentage ⇩ of churches in each category (vertical total 100%) whose **adult attendance** 1985-1989:									
Grew %									33
Remained static %			*Inadequate numbers to give reliable percentages*						67
Declined %									0

[1] Figures sum to more than *100%* because multiple answers were possible

Age and sex of churchgoers 1979 and 1989

Age-Group	Population 1979			Churchgoers in 1979			Churchgoers in 1989[1]			Population 1989		
	Men %	Women %	Total %	Men %	Women %	Total %	Men %	Women %	Total %	Men %	Women %	Total %
Under 15	11	10	21	14	13	27	11	13	24	10	9	19
15-19	4	4	8	5	7	12	3	4	7	4	4	8
20-29	7	7	14	3	3	6	5	7	12	8	8	16
30-44	10	9	19	5	8	13	6	8	14	10	10	20
45-64	11	12	23	9	14	23	11	14	25	11	11	22
65 and over	6	9	15	9	10	19	8	10	18	6	9	15
All ages	49	51	100	45	55	100	44	56	100	49	51	100

[1] This table is based on responses from 26% of all Orthodox churches in England

Church environment

Percentage of all churches 1989 %	City Centre 9	Inner City 20	Council Estate 3	Suburban/ Urban Fringe 29	Separate Town 18	Other built-up area 6	Rural area: Commuter dormitory 12	Rural area: Other 3	ALL Churches 100
Children attending:									
1985	400	1,700	★	400	300	★	★	★	2,800
⇩ 4 years	−50%	+24%	−	−25%	−33%	−	−	−	+4%
1989	200	2,100	★	300	200	★	★	100	2,900
Percentage of total ⇨ %	7	73	0	10	7	0	0	3	100
Adults attending:									
1985	1,000	3,700	★	2,200	1,000	200	200	100	8,400
⇩ 4 years	−10%	−3%	−	+18%	+40%	0%	+100%	+100%	+12%
1989	900	3,600	100	2,600	1,400	200	400	200	9,400
Percentage of total ⇨ %	10	38	1	28	15	2	4	2	100
Membership:									
1985	5,300	158,900	500	45,000	7,100	500	1,700	1,000	220,000
⇩ 4 years	−4%	+2%	0%	+17%	+4%	+40%	+35%	0%	+6%
1989	5,100	162,600	500	52,500	7,400	700	2,300	1,000	232,100
Percentage of total ⇨ %	2	70	0	23	3	0	1	1	100

Percentage ⇩ of churches in each category (vertical total 100%) whose **adult attendance** 1985-1989:		
Grew %		33
Remained static %	*Inadequate numbers to give reliable percentages*	67
Declined %		0

Percentage ⇩ of churches in each category (vertical total 100%) in 1985 whose **services** were held:		
Morning only %		65
Morning & Evening %	*Inadequate numbers to give reliable percentages*	35
Evening only %		0

Percentage ⇩ of churches in each category (vertical total 100%) in 1989 whose **services** were held:		
Morning only %		63
Morning & Evening %	*Inadequate numbers to give reliable percentages*	37
Evening only %		0

Size[1] of church by weekly adult attendance 1979 and 1989[2]

	10 or under	11-25	26-50	51-100	101-150	151-200	201-300	301-400	401-500	Over 500	Average size[1]	Number (=100%)
ALL Churches 1979 %	7	20	30	15	10	9	6	−	3	−	72	97
ALL Churches 1989 %	0	35	23	8	8	11	12	0	3	−	82	114

[1] Total of morning and evening services (when both held) with those attending both times counted twice
[2] This table is based on responses from 33% of all Orthodox churches in 1989

BROAD EVANGELICAL

1989 Broad Evangelical adult church attendance
as percentage of adult population: 0.9%

1989 Broad Evangelical adult church attendance
as percentage of all adult church attendance: 9%

1989 Broad Evangelical child church attendance
as percentage of child population: 1.2%

1989 Broad Evangelical child church attendance
as percentage of all child church attendance: 9%

Denomination of church and people

Percentage of all churches	Metho-dist	Baptist	URC	Inde-pendent	Afro-Carib-bean	Pente-costal	Other	TOTAL Free Churches	Anglican	Roman Catholic	TOTAL Christian
1989 ⇨ %	35	11	6	3	0	0	7	62	38	0	100
Children attending:											
1985	33,600	13,900	3,000	3,200	1,300	300	11,200	66,500	51,400	0	117,900
⇩ 4 years	−15%	−15%	−37%	+19%	−8%	−33%	−14%	−14%	−4%	−	−10%
1989	28,500	11,800	1,900	3,800	1,200	200	9,600	57,000	49,200	0	106,200
Percentage of total ⇨ %	27	11	2	4	1	0	9	54	46	0	100
Adults attending:											
1985	100,500	42,700	3,800	31,500	2,400	500	24,600	206,000	143,100	★	349,100
⇩ 4 years	−7%	−12%	−5%	0%	+13%	+20%	−2%	−6%	+2%	−	−3%
1989	93,900	37,400	3,600	31,600	2,700	600	24,000	193,800	146,500	★	340,300
Percentage of total ⇨ %	28	11	1	9	1	0	7	57	43	0	100
Membership:											
1985	97,500	36,500	20,900	10,500	1,600	400	29,200	196,600	219,300	100	416,000
⇩ 4 years	−4%	−3%	+1%	+67%	−6%	0%	+21%	+4%	−8%	0%	−2%
1989	93,900	35,900	21,100	17,500	1,500	400	35,300	205,100	201,200	100	406,400
Percentage of total ⇨ %	23	9	5	4	0	0	9	50	50	0	100
Percentage ⇩ of churches in each category (vertical total 100%) whose **adult attendance** 1985-1989:											
Grew %	19	25	28	21	−	−	20	22	33	−	24
Remained static %	74	72	64	78	−	−	77	74	63	−	72
Declined %	7	3	8	1	−	−	3	4	4	−	4

Year church/congregation founded

	Before 1500	1500-1799	1800-1849	1850-1874	1875-1899	1900-1924	1925-1949	1950-1974	1975 or later	ALL Churches
Percentage of all churches 1989 ⇨ %	19	7	17	15	19	9	5	6	3	100
Percentage ⇩ of churches in each category (vertical total 100%) whose **adult attendance** 1985-1989:										
Grew %	33	25	21	21	24	25	20	38	36	24
Remained static %	61	67	75	75	71	73	78	51	63	72
Declined %	6	8	4	4	5	2	2	11	1	4

Types of Third World Community Aid church would support

Percentage of all churches 1989 ⇨ %	Project activities	Specific Geographical area	Named communities	Named individuals	Administered through local churches	Evangelism/ missionary work	Other	No support	TOTAL ALL Churches
	40	16	8	19	41	69	1	1	195[1]
Percentage ⇩ of churches in each category (vertical total 100%) whose **adult attendance** 1985-1989:									
Grew %	25	23	29	28	25	22	6	0	24
Remained static %	71	72	65	67	72	75	89	92	72
Declined %	4	5	6	5	3	3	5	8	4

[1] Figures sum to more than 100% because multiple answers were possible

Age and sex of churchgoers 1989

Age-Group	Churchgoers in 1989			Population 1989		
	Men %	Women %	Total %	Men %	Women %	Total %
Under 15	11	13	24	10	9	19
15-19	3	3	6	4	4	8
20-29	4	4	8	8	8	16
30-44	6	10	16	10	10	20
45-64	9	13	22	11	11	22
65 and over	7	17	24	6	9	15
All ages	40	60	100	49	51	100

Church environment

Percentage of all churches 1989 %	City Centre 2	Inner City 5	Council Estate 5	Suburban/ Urban Fringe 24	Separate Town 13	Other built-up area 4	Rural area: Commuter dormitory 16	Rural area: Other 31	ALL Churches 100
Children attending:									
1985	6,200	5,500	6,600	44,000	21,400	6,100	15,100	13,000	117,900
⇩ 4 years	−6%	−16%	−20%	−8%	−11%	−15%	−7%	−9%	−10%
1989	5,800	4,600	5,300	40,400	19,000	5,200	14,100	11,800	106,200
Percentage of total ⇨ %	6	4	5	38	18	5	13	11	100
Adults attending:									
1985	27,900	19,700	14,400	120,700	65,400	17,800	39,900	43,300	349,100
⇩ 4 years	−7%	−6%	−2%	−3%	+2%	−3%	−3%	−3%	−3%
1989	25,900	18,600	14,100	116,700	66,700	17,200	38,900	42,200	340,300
Percentage of total ⇨ %	8	6	4	34	20	5	11	12	100
Membership:									
1985	22,600	20,600	16,500	138,600	86,400	20,600	54,900	55,800	416,000
⇩ 4 years	−3%	−2%	−3%	+3%	−5%	+4%	−9%	−6%	−2%
1989	21,900	20,100	16,000	142,400	81,800	21,500	50,200	52,500	406,400
Percentage of total ⇨ %	6	5	4	35	20	5	12	13	100
Percentage of churches in each category (vertical total 100%) whose **adult attendance** 1985-1989:									
Grew %	28	23	20	27	30	25	20	16	24
Remained static %	58	70	78	70	66	71	76	81	72
Declined %	14	7	2	3	4	4	4	3	4
Percentage of churches in each category (vertical total 100%) in 1985 whose **services** were held:									
Morning only %	†	(24)	(36)	16	18	48	40	46	32
Morning & Evening %	†	(64)	(58)	76	70	40	30	27	50
Evening only %	†	(12)	(6)	8	12	12	30	27	18
Percentage of churches in each category (vertical total 100%) in 1989 whose **services** were held:									
Morning only %	†	(32)	(48)	22	24	64	54	61	43
Morning & Evening %	†	(60)	(48)	72	68	28	26	19	44
Evening only %	†	(8)	(4)	6	8	8	20	20	13

Size[1] of church by weekly adult attendance 1989

	10 or under	11-25	26-50	51- 100	101- 150	151- 200	201- 300	301- 400	401- 500	Over 500	Average size[1]	Number (=100%)
ALL Churches 1989 %	1	5	26	28	20	11	5	2	1	1	91	4,190
Growing churches %	0	0	5	26	29	23	9	4	3	1	137	985
Static churches %	1	7	31	28	17	9	4	1	1	1	81	3,058
Declining churches %	1	6	24	28	25	14	2	—	—	—	78	147

[1] Total of morning and evening services (where both held) with those attending both times counted twice

MAINSTREAM EVANGELICAL

1989 Mainstream Evangelical adult church attendance as percentage of adult population: 0.6%

1989 Mainstream Evangelical adult church attendance as percentage of all adult church attendance: 7%

1989 Mainstream Evangelical child church attendance as percentage of child population: 1.5%

1989 Mainstream Evangelical child church attendance as percentage of all child church attendance: 11%

Denomination of church and people

Percentage of all churches	Metho-dist	Baptist	URC	Inde-pendent	Afro-Carib-bean	Pente-costal	Other	TOTAL Free Churches	Anglican	Roman Catholic	TOTAL Christian
1989 ⇨ %	14	26	2	31	2	3	14	92	8	0	100
Children attending:											
1985	10,100	33,500	2,000	52,000	9,000	3,500	18,000	128,100	13,500	300	141,900
↻ 4 years	−13%	−11%	−20%	−6%	−9%	+26%	−11%	−8%	−21%	+33%	−9%
1989	8,800	29,800	1,600	48,900	8,200	4,400	16,000	117,700	10,600	400	128,700
Percentage of total ⇨ %	7	23	1	38	6	4	13	92	8	0	100
Adults attending:											
1985	16,400	75,300	2,700	64,700	12,200	7,400	40,600	219,300	34,300	2,900	256,500
↻ 4 years	+2%	+5%	−11%	−1%	−14%	0%	−1%	+1%	+15%	−14%	+2%
1989	16,800	79,200	2,400	64,300	10,500	7,400	40,200	220,800	39,500	2,500	262,800
Percentage of total ⇨ %	6	30	1	25	4	3	15	84	15	1	100
Membership:											
1985	41,200	61,800	2,000	51,900	24,400	5,500	45,400	232,200	44,300	7,100	283,600
↻ 4 years	−19%	+1%	0%	+19%	+15%	−9%	−11%	0%	+10%	−4%	+2%
1989	33,200	62,200	2,000	61,700	28,000	5,000	40,500	232,600	48,700	6,800	288,100
Percentage of total ⇨ %	11	22	1	21	10	2	14	81	17	2	100
Percentage ↻ of churches in each category (vertical total 100%) whose **adult attendance** 1985-1989:											
Grew %	10	38	(34)	27	28	7	16	25	28	—	26
Remained static %	79	50	(66)	63	54	80	70	64	57	—	62
Declined %	11	12	(0)	10	18	13	14	11	15	—	12

Year church/congregation founded

		Before 1500	1500-1799	1800-1849	1850-1874	1875-1899	1900-1924	1925-1949	1950-1974	1975 or later	ALL Churches
Percentage of all churches 1989 ⇨ %		3	6	13	13	22	12	13	11	7	100
Percentage ↻ of churches in each category (vertical total 100%) whose **adult attendance** 1985-1989:											
Grew	%	39	36	30	19	24	13	18	39	34	26
Remained static	%	57	64	56	69	60	75	68	51	55	62
Declined	%	4	0	14	12	16	12	14	10	11	12

Types of Third World Community Aid church would support

Percentage of all churches 1989 ⇨ %	Project activities	Specific Geographical area	Named communities	Named individuals	Administered through local churches	Evangelism/ missionary work	Other	No support	TOTAL ALL Churches
	30	13	5	17	31	85	1	1	183[1]
Percentage ↻ of churches in each category (vertical total 100%) whose **adult attendance** 1985-1989:									
Grew %	30	28	26	27	28	24	18	8	26
Remained static %	56	59	54	61	61	65	61	72	62
Declined %	14	13	20	12	11	11	21	20	12

[1] Figures sum to more than 100% because multiple answers were possible

Age and sex of churchgoers 1989

Age-Group	Churchgoers in 1989			Population 1989		
	Men %	Women %	Total %	Men %	Women %	Total %
Under 15	15	18	33	10	9	19
15-19	4	4	8	4	4	8
20-29	4	5	9	8	8	16
30-44	6	8	14	10	10	20
45-64	7	11	18	11	11	22
65 and over	5	13	18	6	9	15
All ages	41	59	100	49	51	100

Church environment

	City Centre	Inner City	Council Estate	Suburban/ Urban Fringe	Separate Town	Other built-up area	Rural area: Commuter dormitory	Rural area: Other	ALL Churches
Percentage of all churches 1989 %	3	9	9	28	15	5	11	20	100
Children attending:									
1985	6,800	12,500	15,400	47,800	23,300	7,300	14,800	14,000	141,900
⇩ 4 years	−16%	−3%	−20%	−5%	−6%	−7%	−13%	−16%	−9%
1989	5,700	12,100	12,300	45,300	21,900	6,800	12,900	11,700	128,700
Percentage of total ⇨ %	5	9	10	35	17	5	10	9	100
Adults attending:									
1985	22,600	27,100	15,400	88,400	43,400	11,700	20,600	27,300	256,500
⇩ 4 years	−3%	0%	+2%	+2%	+8%	+2%	+3%	+3%	+2%
1989	22,000	27,200	15,700	90,100	46,700	11,900	21,200	28,000	262,800
Percentage of total ⇨ %	8	10	6	34	18	5	8	11	100
Membership:									
1985	17,100	28,100	14,700	106,100	49,400	14,300	21,200	32,700	283,600
⇩ 4 years	+7%	+6%	+4%	−4%	+8%	+2%	+12%	−4%	+2%
1989	18,300	29,900	15,300	101,400	53,500	14,600	23,800	31,300	288,100
Percentage of total ⇨ %	6	11	5	35	19	5	8	11	100
Percentage of churches in each category (vertical total 100%) whose **adult attendance** 1985-1989:									
Grew %	30	22	24	27	36	19	29	18	26
Remained static %	54	62	63	58	57	66	60	75	62
Declined %	16	16	13	15	7	15	11	7	12
Percentage of churches in each category (vertical total 100%) in 1985 whose **services** were held:									
Morning only %	(20)	20	15	25	10	20	30	47	30
Morning & Evening %	(70)	75	77	65	78	70	59	35	59
Evening only %	(10)	5	8	10	12	10	11	18	11
Percentage of churches in each category (vertical total 100%) in 1989 whose **services** were held:									
Morning only %	(33)	33	24	41	16	33	47	71	41
Morning & Evening %	(64)	65	74	56	80	64	5	21	55
Evening only %	(3)	2	2	3	4	3	3	8	4

Size[1] of church by weekly adult attendance 1989

	10 or under	11-25	26-50	51- 100	101- 150	151- 200	201- 300	301- 400	401- 500	Over 500	Average size[1]	Number (=100%)
ALL Churches 1989 %	1	9	33	26	20	7	2	1	½	½	71	4,344
Growing churches %	0	0	23	22	33	13	4	2	1	1	102	1,108
Static churches %	1	11	39	26	14	7	1	1	−	−	66	2,736
Declining churches %	2	19	19	32	22	3	1	1	1	−	65	500

[1] Total of morning and evening services (where both held) with those attending both times counted twice

CHARISMATIC EVANGELICAL

1989 Charismatic Evangelical adult church attendance
as percentage of adult population: *1.1%*

1989 Charismatic Evangelical adult church attendance
as percentage of all adult church attendance: *12%*

1989 Charismatic Evangelical child church attendance
as percentage of child population: *2.2%*

1989 Charismatic Evangelical child church attendance
as percentage of all child church attendance: *16%*

Denomination of church and people

Percentage of all churches 1989 ⇨ %	Metho-dist	Baptist	URC	Inde-pendent	Afro-Carib-bean	Pente-costal	Other	TOTAL Free Churches	Anglican	Roman Catholic	TOTAL Christian
	7	*13*	*1*	*27*	*6*	*16*	*1*	*71*	*29*	*0*	*100*
Children attending:											
1985	9,000	23,700	5,700	43,300	26,000	30,700	1,700	140,100	53,500	600	194,200
⇩ 4 years	−8%	−2%	−9%	+25%	−6%	+3%	−6%	+6%	−5%	−33%	+3%
1989	8,300	23,200	5,200	54,200	24,400	31,700	1,600	148,600	50,900	400	199,900
Percentage of total ⇨ %	*4*	*12*	*2*	*27*	*12*	*16*	*1*	*74*	*26*	*0*	*100*
Adults attending:											
1985	16,300	39,000	5,900	96,700	43,300	74,600	3,200	279,000	113,300	2,500	394,800
⇩ 4 years	−7%	+13%	+24%	+19%	+7%	+12%	+3%	+13%	−6%	+36%	+7%
1989	15,200	43,900	7,300	115,200	46,300	83,300	3,300	314,500	106,200	3,400	424,100
Percentage of total ⇨ %	*3*	*10*	*2*	*27*	*11*	*20*	*1*	*74*	*25*	*1*	*100*
Membership:											
1985	22,300	47,600	5,100	61,800	25,700	52,000	3,800	218,300	167,000	13,100	398,400
⇩ 4 years	+6%	+9%	+4%	+27%	+7%	+13%	−8%	+14%	−7%	+17%	+6%
1989	23,600	52,100	5,300	78,500	27,600	58,700	3,500	249,300	155,800	15,300	420,400
Percentage of total ⇨ %	*5*	*12*	*1*	*19*	*7*	*14*	*1*	*59*	*37*	*4*	*100*
Percentage ⇩ of churches in each category (vertical total 100%) whose **adult attendance** 1985-1989:											
Grew %	26	49	29	51	32	38	28	42	40	−	41
Remained static %	62	45	62	43	62	56	55	51	53	−	52
Declined %	12	6	9	6	6	6	17	7	7	−	7

Year church/congregation founded

	Before 1500	1500-1799	1800-1849	1850-1874	1875-1899	1900-1924	1925-1949	1950-1974	1975 or later	ALL Churches
Percentage of all churches 1989 ⇨ %	9	3	9	6	10	7	13	16	27	100
Percentage ⇩ of churches in each category (vertical total 100%) whose **adult attendance** 1985-1989:										
Grew %	39	35	46	28	38	42	40	39	54	41
Remained static %	56	62	46	62	54	50	54	53	41	52
Declined %	5	3	8	10	8	8	6	8	5	7

Types of Third World Community Aid church would support

Percentage of all churches 1989 ⇨ %	Project activities	Specific Geographical area	Named communities	Named individuals	Administered through local churches	Evangelism/missionary work	Other	No support	TOTAL ALL Churches
	27	*22*	*7*	*23*	*36*	*82*	*1*	*1*	*199*[1]
Percentage ⇩ of churches in each category (vertical total 100%) whose **adult attendance** 1985-1989:									
Grew %	40	37	42	48	42	40	51	70	41
Remained static %	52	53	50	48	52	53	44	15	52
Declined %	8	10	8	4	6	7	5	15	7

[1] Figures sum to more than *100%* because multiple answers were possible

Age and sex of churchgoers 1989

Age-Group	Churchgoers in 1989			Population 1989		
	Men %	Women %	Total %	Men %	Women %	Total %
Under 15	14	18	32	10	9	19
15-19	3	5	8	4	4	8
20-29	6	7	13	8	8	16
30-44	9	11	20	10	10	20
45-64	7	10	17	11	11	22
65 and over	3	7	10	6	9	15
All ages	42	58	100	49	51	100

Church environment

	City Centre	Inner City	Council Estate	Suburban/ Urban Fringe	Separate Town	Other built-up area	Rural area: Commuter dormitory	Rural area: Other	ALL Churches
Percentage of all churches 1989 %	2	12	10	29	18	6	12	11	100
Children attending:									
1985	4,300	19,000	18,800	75,000	35,300	8,700	22,200	10,900	194,200
⬦ 4 years	+33%	+12%	−4%	+2%	+2%	+29%	−6%	−3%	+3%
1989	5,700	21,200	18,000	76,400	36,000	11,200	20,800	10,600	199,900
Percentage of total ⬦ %	3	11	9	38	18	6	10	5	100
Adults attending:									
1985	19,300	53,000	27,700	145,900	68,000	21,000	38,000	21,900	394,800
⬦ 4 years	+2%	+5%	+7%	+7%	+13%	+7%	+8%	+7%	+7%
1989	19,700	55,700	29,700	155,600	76,600	22,400	40,900	23,500	424,100
Percentage of total ⬦ %	5	13	7	37	18	5	10	5	100
Membership:									
1985	31,100	48,400	25,300	159,700	74,500	17,500	39,300	20,600	398,400
⬦ 4 years	+24%	+11%	+8%	+5%	+2%	+15%	−1%	+2%	+6%
1989	16,300	53,700	27,200	166,900	76,000	20,200	39,100	21,000	420,400
Percentage of total ⬦ %	4	13	6	40	18	5	9	5	100
Percentage of churches in each category (vertical total 100%) whose **adult attendance** 1985-1989:									
Grew %	49	44	39	37	46	46	44	32	41
Remained static %	44	46	51	57	45	48	51	66	52
Declined %	7	10	10	6	9	6	5	2	7
Percentage of churches in each category (vertical total 100%) in 1985 whose **services** were held:									
Morning only %	(40)	30	20	16	20	(55)	52	52	30
Morning & Evening %	(30)	64	62	79	74	(25)	26	33	58
Evening only %	(30)	6	18	5	6	(20)	22	25	12
Percentage of churches in each category (vertical total 100%) in 1989 whose **services** were held:									
Morning only %	(45)	37	25	20	28	35	38	45	30
Morning & Evening %	(30)	48	69	79	72	48	50	37	62
Evening only %	(25)	15	6	1	0	17	12	18	8

Size[1] of church by weekly adult attendance 1989

	10 or under	11-25	26-50	51-100	101-150	151-200	201-300	301-400	401-500	Over 500	Average size[1]	Number (=100%)
ALL Churches 1989 %	1	6	22	25	23	15	5	1	1	1	95	5,107
Growing churches %	0	1	15	22	30	20	8	2	1	1	117	2,069
Static churches %	1	10	26	26	18	12	5	1	1/2	1/2	82	2,706
Declining churches %	2	7	23	37	26	2	2	1/2	1/2	—	68	332

[1] Total of morning and evening services (where both held) with those attending both times counted twice

TOTAL EVANGELICAL

1989 Total Evangelical adult church attendance
as percentage of adult population: 2.6%

1989 Total Evangelical adult church attendance
as percentage of all adult church attendance: 28%

1989 Total Evangelical child church attendance
as percentage of child population: 4.9%

1989 Total Evangelical child church attendance
as percentage of all child church attendance: 36%

Denomination of church and people

Percentage of all churches	Metho-dist	Baptist	URC	Inde-pendent	Afro-Carib-bean	Pente-costal	Other	TOTAL Free Churches	Anglican	Roman Catholic	TOTAL Christian
1989 ⇨ %	18	17	3	20	3	7	7	75	25	0	100
Children attending:											
1985	52,700	71,100	10,700	98,500	36,300	34,500	30,900	334,700	118,400	900	454,000
⇩ 4 years	−13%	−9%	−19%	+9%	−7%	+5%	−12%	−3%	−7%	−11%	−4%
1989	45,600	64,800	8,700	106,900	33,800	36,300	27,200	323,300	110,200	800	434,800
Percentage of total ⇨ %	11	15	2	25	8	8	6	75	25	0	100
Adults attending:											
1985	133,200	157,000	12,400	192,900	57,900	82,500	68,400	704,300	290,700	5,400	1,000,400
⇩ 4 years	−5%	+2%	+7%	+9%	+3%	+11%	−1%	+4%	+1%	+9%	+3%
1989	125,900	160,500	13,300	211,100	59,500	91,300	67,500	729,100	292,200	5,900	1,027,200
Percentage of total ⇨ %	12	15	1	21	6	9	7	71	28	1	100
Membership:											
1985	161,000	145,900	28,000	124,200	51,700	57,900	78,400	647,100	430,600	20,300	1,098,000
⇩ 4 years	−6%	+3%	+1%	+27%	+10%	+11%	+1%	+6%	−6%	+9%	+2%
1989	150,700	149,700	28,400	157,700	57,100	64,100	79,300	687,000	405,700	22,200	1,114,900
Percentage of total ⇨ %	14	13	3	14	5	6	7	62	36	2	100
Percentage ⇩ of churches in each category (vertical total 100%) whose **adult attendance** 1985-1989:											
Grew %	19	35	29	30	32	34	19	28	35	−	30
Remained static %	72	59	63	65	62	59	72	65	58	−	63
Declined %	9	6	8	5	6	7	9	7	7	−	7

Year church/congregation founded

	Before 1500	1500-1799	1800-1849	1850-1874	1875-1899	1900-1924	1925-1949	1950-1974	1975 or later	ALL Churches
Percentage of all churches 1989 ⇨ %	10	5	13	11	17	9	11	11	13	100
Percentage ⇩ of churches in each category (vertical total 100%) whose **adult attendance** 1985-1989:										
Grew %	36	29	30	22	27	27	28	32	46	30
Remained static %	59	66	63	70	64	67	66	61	49	63
Declined %	5	5	7	8	9	6	6	7	5	7

Types of Third World Community Aid church would support

	Project activities	Specific Geographical area	Named communities	Named individuals	Administered through local churches	Evangelism/ missionary work	Other	No support	TOTAL ALL Churches
Percentage of all churches 1989 ⇨ %	31	17	7	19	35	76	1	1	187[1]
Percentage ⇩ of churches in each category (vertical total 100%) whose **adult attendance** 1985-1989:									
Grew %	22	29	30	35	31	29	25	26	30
Remained static %	72	62	60	59	63	65	67	60	63
Declined %	6	9	10	6	6	6	8	14	7

[1] Figures sum to more than 100% because multiple answers were possible

Age and sex of churchgoers 1989

Age-Group	Churchgoers in 1989			Population 1989		
	Men %	Women %	Total %	Men %	Women %	Total %
Under 15	13	17	30	10	9	19
15-19	3	4	7	4	4	8
20-29	4	6	10	8	8	16
30-44	8	10	18	10	10	20
45-64	8	10	18	11	11	22
65 and over	5	12	17	6	9	15
All ages	41	59	100	49	51	100

Church environment

	City Centre	Inner City	Council Estate	Suburban/ Urban Fringe	Separate Town	Other built-up area	Rural area: Commuter dormitory	Rural area: Other	ALL Churches
Percentage of all churches 1989 %	2	9	8	27	15	5	13	21	100
Children attending:									
1985	17,300	37,000	40,800	166,800	80,000	22,100	52,100	37,900	454,000
⇩ 4 years	−1%	+2%	−13%	−3%	−4%	+5%	−8%	−10%	−4%
1989	17,200	37,900	35,600	162,100	76,900	23,200	47,800	34,100	434,800
Percentage of total ⇨ %	4	9	8	37	18	5	11	8	100
Adults attending:									
1985	69,800	99,800	57,500	355,000	176,800	50,500	98,500	92,500	1,000,400
⇩ 4 years	−3%	+2%	+3%	+2%	+7%	+2%	+3%	+1%	+3%
1989	67,600	101,500	59,500	362,400	190,000	51,500	101,000	93,700	1,027,200
Percentage of total ⇨ %	7	10	6	35	18	5	10	9	100
Membership:									
1985	52,800	97,100	56,500	404,400	210,300	52,400	115,400	109,100	1,098,000
⇩ 4 years	+7%	+7%	+4%	+2%	0%	+7%	−2%	−4%	+2%
1989	56,500	103,700	58,500	410,700	211,300	56,300	113,100	104,800	1,114,900
Percentage of total ⇨ %	5	9	5	37	19	5	10	10	100

Percentage of churches in each category (vertical total 100%) whose **adult attendance** 1985-1989:

	City Centre	Inner City	Council Estate	Suburban/ Urban Fringe	Separate Town	Other built-up area	Rural area: Commuter dormitory	Rural area: Other	ALL Churches
Grew %	35	33	29	31	37	31	30	21	31
Remained static %	52	56	63	62	56	62	64	75	62
Declined %	13	11	8	7	7	7	6	4	7

Percentage of churches in each category (vertical total 100%) in 1985 whose **services** were held:

	City Centre	Inner City	Council Estate	Suburban/ Urban Fringe	Separate Town	Other built-up area	Rural area: Commuter dormitory	Rural area: Other	ALL Churches
Morning only %	(27)	25	19	20	15	38	40	48	30
Morning & Evening %	(56)	69	69	72	75	48	40	30	57
Evening only %	(17)	6	12	8	10	14	20	22	13

Percentage of churches in each category (vertical total 100%) in 1989 whose **services** were held:

	City Centre	Inner City	Council Estate	Suburban/ Urban Fringe	Separate Town	Other built-up area	Rural area: Commuter dormitory	Rural area: Other	ALL Churches
Morning only %	(38)	35	27	30	22	39	46	63	38
Morning & Evening %	(52)	57	69	67	75	52	44	23	55
Evening only %	(10)	8	4	3	3	9	10	14	7

Size[1] of church by weekly adult attendance 1989

	10 or under	11-25	26-50	51-100	101-150	151-200	201-300	301-400	401-500	Over 500	Average size[1]	Number (=100%)
ALL Churches 1989 %	1	8	26	25	21	12	4	1	1	1	87	13,641
Growing churches %	0	0	16	23	31	19	7	2	1	1	115	4,162
Static churches %	1	10	33	26	16	9	2	1	1	1	75	8,500
Declining churches %	2	13	21	33	24	4	1	1	1	−	69	979

[1] Total of morning and evening services (where both held) with those attending both times counted twice

LOW CHURCH

1989 Low Church adult church attendance
as percentage of adult population: 0.6%

1989 Low Church adult church attendance
as percentage of all adult church attendance: 6%

1989 Low Church child church attendance
as percentage of child population: 0.8%

1989 Low Church child church attendance
as percentage of all child church attendance: 6%

Denomination of church and people

Percentage of all churches 1989 ⇨ %	Metho-dist	Baptist	URC	Inde-pendent	Afro-Carib-bean	Pente-costal	Other	TOTAL Free Churches	Anglican	Roman Catholic	TOTAL Christian[1]
	36	2	6	3	0	0	2	49	51	0	100
Children attending:											
1985	25,600	2,400	6,800	4,300	400	100	1,500	41,100	32,700	200	74,000
⇩ 4 years	−19%	−8%	−24%	+21%	−25%	+100%	−13%	−14%	−1%	0%	−8%
1989	20,800	2,200	5,200	5,200	300	200	1,300	35,200	32,500	200	67,900
Percentage of total ⇨ %	31	3	8	8	0	0	2	52	48	0	100
Adults attending:											
1985	74,800	6,800	19,300	6,700	400	200	4,100	112,300	130,800	400	243,500
⇩ 4 years	+2%	+4%	−9%	+22%	−25%	+200%	+17%	+2%	−9%	−50%	−4%
1989	76,600	7,100	17,500	8,200	300	600	4,800	115,100	118,400	200	233,700
Percentage of total ⇨ %	33	3	7	4	0	0	2	49	51	0	100
Membership:											
1985	81,700	5,300	17,500	7,100	200	400	5,200	117,400	191,900	500	309,800
⇩ 4 years	−5%	+4%	−7%	+6%	−50%	+25%	+8%	−3%	−3%	0%	−3%
1989	78,000	5,500	16,300	7,500	100	500	5,600	113,500	186,600	500	300,800
Percentage of total ⇨ %	26	2	6	2	0	0	2	38	62	0	100
Percentage ⇩ of churches in each category (vertical total 100%) whose **adult attendance** 1985-1989:											
Grew %	14	26	13	26	–	–	20	16	24	–	20
Remained static %	76	69	77	67	–	–	75	75	67	–	71
Declined %	10	5	10	7	–	–	5	9	9	–	9

[1] This column includes Orthodox Church figures for child attendance of 0 and 0; adult attendance figures of ★ and ★; and membership figures of ★ and 200 respectively for 1985 and 1989 with one congregation in 1989

Year church/congregation founded

	Before 1500	1500-1799	1800-1849	1850-1874	1875-1899	1900-1924	1925-1949	1950-1974	1975 or later	ALL Churches
Percentage of all churches 1989 ⇨ %	29	7	15	15	15	8	5	5	1	100
Percentage ⇩ of churches in each category (vertical total 100%) whose **adult attendance** 1985-1989:										
Grew %	23	14	17	21	21	19	14	27	25	20
Remained static %	67	81	75	69	71	70	75	64	59	71
Declined %	10	5	8	10	8	11	11	9	16	9

Types of Third World Community Aid church would support

Percentage of all churches 1989 ⇨ %	Project activities	Specific Geographical area	Named communities	Named individuals	Administered through local churches	Evangelism/ missionary work	Other	No support	TOTAL ALL Churches
	40	15	9	16	37	50	1	5	173[1]
Percentage ⇩ of churches in each category (vertical total 100%) whose **adult attendance** 1985-1989:									
Grew %	24	14	12	20	15	28	9	0	20
Remained static %	71	74	75	71	71	64	89	100	71
Declined %	5	12	13	9	14	8	2	0	9

[1] Figures sum to more than 100% because multiple answers were possible

Age and sex of churchgoers 1989

Age-Group	Churchgoers in 1989			Population 1989		
	Men %	Women %	Total %	Men %	Women %	Total %
Under 15	10	13	23	10	9	19
15-19	2	3	5	4	4	8
20-29	3	4	7	8	8	16
30-44	5	9	14	10	10	20
45-64	9	15	24	11	11	22
65 and over	8	19	27	6	9	15
All ages	37	63	100	49	51	100

Church environment

Percentage of all churches 1989 %	City Centre 1	Inner City 4	Council Estate 4	Suburban/ Urban Fringe 16	Separate Town 6	Other built-up area 4	Rural area: Commuter dormitory 18	Rural area: Other 47	ALL Churches 100
Children attending:									
1985	1,900	4,000	4,200	23,200	7,700	3,600	12,800	16,600	74,000
⇩ 4 years	−5%	−5%	0%	−12%	−5%	+6%	−5%	−13%	−8%
1989	1,800	3,800	4,200	20,400	7,300	3,800	12,200	14,400	67,900
Percentage of total ⇨ %	3	5	6	30	11	5	18	22	100
Adults attending:									
1985	6,300	14,000	10,900	72,500	26,000	14,000	36,200	63,600	243,500
⇩ 4 years	−8%	−6%	−4%	−5%	+1%	−4%	−4%	−4%	−4%
1989	5,800	13,200	10,500	68,900	26,200	13,400	34,700	61,000	233,700
Percentage of total ⇨ %	2	6	4	30	11	6	15	26	100
Membership:									
1985	5,800	15,700	11,200	92,100	40,100	18,600	50,400	75,900	309,800
⇩ 4 years	+10%	−8%	−5%	+6%	−8%	−13%	−2%	−9%	−3%
1989	6,400	14,500	10,600	98,000	37,000	16,100	49,300	68,900	300,800
Percentage of total ⇨ %	2	5	4	33	12	5	16	23	100
Percentage of churches in each category (vertical total 100%) whose **adult attendance** 1985-1989:									
Grew %	(14)	23	22	21	25	23	20	16	20
Remained static %	(50)	63	72	68	66	64	75	78	71
Declined %	(36)	14	6	11	9	13	5	6	9
Percentage of churches in each category (vertical total 100%) in 1985 whose **services** were held:									
Morning only %	(20)	10	37	30	23	20	49	49	40
Morning & Evening %	(75)	78	43	66	73	64	39	28	44
Evening only %	(5)	12	20	4	4	16	12	23	16
Percentage of churches in each category (vertical total 100%) in 1989 whose **services** were held:									
Morning only %	(25)	12	45	37	28	28	59	58	49
Morning & Evening %	(70)	78	38	60	69	56	31	21	37
Evening only %	(5)	10	17	3	3	16	10	21	14

Size[1] of church by weekly adult attendance 1989

	10 or under	11-25	26-50	51- 100	101- 150	151- 200	201- 300	301- 400	401- 500	Over 500	Average size[1]	Number (=100%)
ALL Churches 1989 %	5	19	22	30	15	7	1½	½	−	−	58	4,441
Growing churches %	0	3	9	36	39	10	2	½	⌐——— ½ ———⌐		91	888
Static churches %	5	24	26	28	8	6	1½	½	−	−	50	3,153
Declining churches %	12	20	22	28	15	3	−	−	−	−	46	400

[1] Total of morning and evening services (where both held) with those attending both times counted twice

BROAD

1989 Broad adult church attendance
as percentage of adult population: *1.0%*

1989 Broad adult church attendance
as percentage of all adult church attendance: *10%*

1989 Broad child church attendance
as percentage of child population: *1.1%*

1989 Broad child church attendance
as percentage of all child church attendance: *8%*

Denomination of church and people

Percentage of all churches 1989 ⇨ %	Metho-dist	Baptist	URC	Inde-pendent	Afro-Carib-bean	Pente-costal	Other	TOTAL Free Churches	Anglican	Roman Catholic	TOTAL Christian[1]
	24	*2*	*5*	*2*	*0*	*0*	*2*	*35*	*65*	*0*	*100*
Children attending:											
1985	31,500	2,300	7,400	4,700	100	100	700	46,800	61,200	900	108,900
⇩ *4 years*	*−16%*	*−4%*	*−11%*	*+36%*	*+100%*	*0%*	*−14%*	*−9%*	*−4%*	*+11%*	*−6%*
1989	26,400	2,200	6,600	6,400	200	100	600	42,500	58,700	1,000	102,200
Percentage of total ⇨ %	*26*	*2*	*7*	*6*	*0*	*0*	*1*	*42*	*57*	*1*	*100*
Adults attending:											
1985	113,400	12,700	25,500	15,500	300	200	2,800	170,400	217,500	1,600	389,800
⇩ *4 years*	*−15%*	*−2%*	*−2%*	*+25%*	*0%*	*+100%*	*+36%*	*−7%*	*−4%*	*+25%*	*−5%*
1989	96,900	12,400	25,000	19,300	300	400	3,800	158,100	209,400	2,000	369,900
Percentage of total ⇨ %	*26*	*4*	*7*	*5*	*0*	*0*	*1*	*43*	*57*	*0*	*100*
Membership:											
1985	97,400	5,500	23,400	21,900	2,200	200	6,200	156,800	339,300	12,200	511,500
⇩ *4 years*	*0%*	*−5%*	*−8%*	*−40%*	*−45%*	*+100%*	*0%*	*−8%*	*−3%*	*+24%*	*−4%*
1989	97,200	5,200	21,600	13,200	1,200	400	6,200	145,000	330,000	15,100	493,400
Percentage of total ⇨ %	*20*	*1*	*5*	*3*	*0*	*0*	*1*	*30*	*67*	*3*	*100*
Percentage ⇩ of churches in each category (vertical total 100%) whose **adult attendance** 1985-1989:											
Grew %	15	23	26	(26)	—	—	(54)	19	26	—	23
Remained static %	71	68	65	(74)	—	—	(36)	69	67	—	68
Declined %	14	9	9	(0)	—	—	(10)	12	7	—	9

[1] This column includes Orthodox Church figures for child attendance of ★ and ★; adult attendance figures of 300 and 400; and membership figures of 3,200 and 3,300 for 1985 and 1989 respectively with 3 congregations in 1989

Year church/congregation founded

	Before 1500	1500-1799	1800-1849	1850-1874	1875-1899	1900-1924	1925-1949	1950-1974	1975 or later	ALL Churches
Percentage of all churches 1989 ⇨ %	*44*	*6*	*11*	*11*	*11*	*7*	*4*	*5*	*1*	*100*
Percentage ⇩ of churches in each category (vertical total 100%) whose **adult attendance** 1985-1989:										
Grew %	23	23	26	27	22	14	22	11	34	23
Remained static %	70	67	63	62	71	73	76	75	48	68
Declined %	7	10	11	11	7	13	2	14	18	9

Types of Third World Community Aid church would support

Percentage of all churches 1989 ⇨ %	Project activities	Specific Geographical area	Named communities	Named individuals	Administered through local churches	Evangelism/ missionary work	Other	No support	TOTAL ALL Churches
	45	*20*	*12*	*16*	*40*	*42*	*1*	*4*	*180*[1]
Percentage ⇩ of churches in each category (vertical total 100%) whose **adult attendance** 1985-1989:									
Grew %	27	23	24	21	19	24	10	19	23
Remained static %	64	67	74	70	72	66	76	72	68
Declined %	9	10	2	9	9	10	14	9	9

[1] Figures sum to more than *100%* because multiple answers were possible

Age and sex of churchgoers 1989

Age-Group	Churchgoers in 1989			Population 1989		
	Men %	Women %	Total %	Men %	Women %	Total %
Under 15	10	12	22	10	9	19
15-19	2	3	5	4	4	8
20-29	3	4	7	8	8	16
30-44	6	9	15	10	10	20
45-64	9	16	25	11	11	22
65 and over	9	17	26	6	9	15
All ages	39	61	100	49	51	100

Church environment

Percentage of all churches 1989 %	City Centre 1	Inner City 2	Council Estate 3	Suburban/ Urban Fringe 16	Separate Town 8	Other built-up area 3	Rural area: Commuter dormitory 21	Rural area: Other 46	ALL Churches 100
Children attending:									
1985	3,100	2,300	4,400	37,400	15,600	4,100	25,100	16,900	108,900
⇩ 4 years	−23%	+9%	−2%	−9%	−10%	−7%	−6%	+4%	−6%
1989	2,400	2,500	4,300	34,000	14,000	3,800	23,600	17,600	102,200
Percentage of total ⇨ %	2	3	4	33	14	4	23	17	100
Adults attending:									
1985	15,900	14,600	16,600	119,000	54,200	14,400	72,100	83,000	389,800
⇩ 4 years	−9%	−6%	−6%	−6%	−1%	−6%	−5%	−5%	−5%
1989	14,400	13,700	15,600	111,900	53,900	13,500	68,300	78,600	369,900
Percentage of total ⇨ %	4	4	4	30	15	4	18	21	100
Membership:									
1985	17,700	14,000	22,700	145,700	76,900	16,700	106,900	110,900	511,500
⇩ 4 years	−9%	+1%	+9%	−3%	+1%	−7%	−7%	−6%	−4%
1989	16,100	14,200	24,800	141,500	77,800	15,600	99,700	103,700	493,400
Percentage of total ⇨ %	3	3	5	29	16	3	20	21	100
Percentage of churches in each category (vertical total 100%) whose **adult attendance** 1985-1989:									
Grew %	(15)	(29)	24	25	29	22	26	15	23
Remained static %	(70)	(64)	70	65	62	69	66	75	68
Declined %	(15)	(7)	6	10	9	9	8	10	9
Percentage of churches in each category (vertical total 100%) in 1985 whose **services** were held:									
Morning only %	†	10	84	28	19	(30)	39	55	44
Morning & Evening %	†	84	11	68	76	(64)	43	17	38
Evening only %	†	6	5	4	5	(6)	18	28	18
Percentage of churches in each category (vertical total 100%) in 1989 whose **services** were held:									
Morning only %	†	12	87	34	23	39	48	64	52
Morning & Evening %	†	83	9	63	73	56	37	13	33
Evening only %	†	5	4	3	4	5	15	23	15

Size[1] of church by weekly adult attendance 1989

	10 or under	11-25	26-50	51-100	101-150	151-200	201-300	301-400	401-500	Over 500	Average size[1]	Number (=100%)
ALL Churches 1989 %	1	13	26	31	21	4	2	1½	½	−	68	6,056
Growing churches %	0	1	16	34	33	10	4	1	½	½	93	1,393
Static churches %	1	18	28	29	18	2	2	1½	½	−	61	4,118
Declining churches %	3	17	23	37	16	2	1½	½	−	−	55	545

[1] Total of morning and evening services (where both held) with those attending both times counted twice

LIBERAL

1989 Liberal adult church attendance
as percentage of adult population: *1.1%*

1989 Liberal adult church attendance
as percentage of all adult church attendance: *11%*

1989 Liberal child church attendance
as percentage of child population: *1.3%*

1989 Liberal child church attendance
as percentage of all child church attendance: *9%*

Denomination of church and people

Percentage of all churches	Metho-dist	Baptist	URC	Inde-pendent	Afro-Carib-bean	Pente-costal	Other	TOTAL Free Churches	Anglican	Roman Catholic	TOTAL Christian
1989 ⇨ %	20	2	11	4	0	0	3	40	59	1	100
Children attending:											
1985	24,900	2,000	16,900	7,000	400	★	1,600	52,800	66,700	600	120,100
⇩ 4 years	−18%	−5%	−17%	+7%	0%	−	−31%	−14%	+1%	+50%	−5%
1989	20,500	1,900	14,000	7,500	400	100	1,100	45,500	67,100	900	113,500
Percentage of total ⇨ %	18	2	12	7	0	0	1	40	59	1	100
Adults attending:											
1985	85,900	18,200	61,300	14,500	1,200	★	4,600	185,700	231,300	9,500	426,500
⇩ 4 years	−5%	−2%	−11%	+17%	−8%	−	+9%	−4%	−3%	−4%	−4%
1989	81,900	17,800	54,600	16,900	1,100	200	5,000	177,500	223,300	9,100	409,900
Percentage of total ⇨ %	20	4	14	4	0	0	1	43	55	2	100
Membership:											
1985	81,300	7,300	53,900	18,200	700	★	8,900	170,300	345,100	39,900	555,300
⇩ 4 years	0%	−1%	−9%	+1%	−14%	−	−1%	−3%	−7%	+23%	−3%
1989	81,400	7,200	49,200	18,300	600	200	8,800	165,700	322,200	49,000	536,900
Percentage of total ⇨ %	15	1	9	4	0	0	2	31	60	9	100

Percentage ⇩ of churches in each category (vertical total 100%) whose **adult attendance** 1985-1989:

	Metho-dist	Baptist	URC	Inde-pendent	Afro-Carib-bean	Pente-costal	Other	TOTAL Free Churches	Anglican	Roman Catholic	TOTAL Christian
Grew %	17	17	16	21	−	−	5	17	29	(39)	24
Remained static %	71	78	72	74	−	−	85	72	65	(61)	68
Declined %	12	5	12	5	−	−	10	11	6	(0)	8

Year church/congregation founded

	Before 1500	1500-1799	1800-1849	1850-1874	1875-1899	1900-1924	1925-1949	1950-1974	1975 or later	ALL Churches
Percentage of all churches 1989 ⇨ %	32	8	13	11	13	8	6	7	2	100

Percentage ⇩ of churches in each category (vertical total 100%) whose **adult attendance** 1985-1989:

	Before 1500	1500-1799	1800-1849	1850-1874	1875-1899	1900-1924	1925-1949	1950-1974	1975 or later	ALL Churches
Grew %	29	19	25	22	19	17	23	24	14	24
Remained static %	67	75	63	75	70	72	68	68	66	68
Declined %	4	6	12	3	11	11	9	8	20	8

Types of Third World Community Aid church would support

Percentage of all churches 1989 ⇨ %	Project activities	Specific Geographical area	Named communities	Named individuals	Administered through local churches	Evangelism/ missionary work	Other	No support	TOTAL ALL Churches
	51	22	16	17	44	38	1	2	191[1]

Percentage ⇩ of churches in each category (vertical total 100%) whose **adult attendance** 1985-1989:

	Project activities	Specific Geographical area	Named communities	Named individuals	Administered through local churches	Evangelism/ missionary work	Other	No support	TOTAL ALL Churches
Grew %	23	26	30	23	23	23	38	22	24
Remained static %	69	70	64	66	68	68	53	61	68
Declined %	8	4	6	11	9	9	9	17	8

[1] Figures sum to more than *100%* because multiple answers were possible

Age and sex of churchgoers 1989

Age-Group	Churchgoers in 1989			Population 1989		
	Men %	Women %	Total %	Men %	Women %	Total %
Under 15	10	12	22	10	9	19
15-19	3	3	6	4	4	8
20-29	3	5	8	8	8	16
30-44	6	9	15	10	10	20
45-64	9	15	24	11	11	22
65 and over	8	17	25	6	9	15
All ages	39	61	100	49	51	100

Church environment

Percentage of all churches 1989 %	City Centre 2	Inner City 6	Council Estate 5	Suburban/ Urban Fringe 28	Separate Town 12	Other built-up area 4	Rural area: Commuter dormitory 19	Rural area: Other 24	ALL Churches 100
Children attending:									
1985	3,800	5,800	5,500	50,000	20,900	5,800	18,200	10,100	120,100
⇩ 4 years	+11%	+2%	+7%	−10%	−10%	−5%	+1%	−1%	−5%
1989	4,200	5,900	5,900	44,800	18,900	5,500	18,300	10,000	113,500
Percentage of total ⇨ %	4	5	5	39	17	5	16	9	100
Adults attending:									
1985	24,600	27,700	17,500	170,000	69,400	18,200	56,600	42,500	426,500
⇩ 4 years	−8%	−6%	−4%	−5%	+1%	−4%	−4%	−4%	−4%
1989	22,600	26,000	16,800	161,900	70,000	17,500	54,300	40,800	409,900
Percentage of total ⇨ %	6	6	4	40	17	4	13	10	100
Membership:									
1985	21,500	25,800	28,800	231,400	97,100	25,200	76,100	49,400	555,300
⇩ 4 years	−1%	+2%	−8%	−1%	−8%	−3%	−3%	−6%	−3%
1989	21,200	26,400	26,600	228,600	89,400	24,400	73,700	46,600	536,900
Percentage of total ⇨ %	4	5	5	42	17	4	14	9	100
Percentage of churches in each category (vertical total 100%) whose **adult attendance** 1985-1989:									
Grew %	(29)	21	25	24	28	17	29	18	24
Remained static %	(63)	70	71	67	64	70	64	77	68
Declined %	(8)	9	4	9	8	13	7	5	8
Percentage of churches in each category (vertical total 100%) in 1985 whose **services** were held:									
Morning only %	†	62	82	10	16	44	20	44	39
Morning & Evening %	†	38	9	88	84	44	75	27	51
Evening only %	†	0	9	2	0	12	5	29	10
Percentage of churches in each category (vertical total 100%) in 1989 whose **services** were held:									
Morning only %	(10)	66	71	17	13	46	28	48	35
Morning & Evening %	(90)	34	22	81	86	51	65	19	51
Evening only %	(0)	0	7	2	1	3	7	33	14

Size[1] of church by weekly adult attendance 1989

	10 or under	11-25	26-50	51- 100	101- 150	151- 200	201- 300	301- 400	401- 500	Over 500	Average size[1]	Number (=100%)
ALL Churches 1989 %	1	11	16	27	24	14	6	1	—	—	87	5,258
Growing churches %	0	0	12	21	30	26	8	2	½	½	120	1,262
Static churches %	1	15	19	27	22	11	4	½	½	—	78	3,575
Declining churches %	3	12	14	42	23	3	2	1	—	—	67	421

[1] Total of morning and evening services (where both held) with those attending both times counted twice

ANGLO-CATHOLIC

1989 Anglo-Catholic adult church attendance
as percentage of adult population: **0.4%**

1989 Anglo-Catholic adult church attendance
as percentage of all adult church attendance: **4%**

1989 Anglo-Catholic child church attendance
as percentage of child population: **0.4%**

1989 Anglo-Catholic child church attendance
as percentage of all child church attendance: **3%**

Denomination of church and people

Percentage of all churches 1989 ⇨ %	Metho-dist	Baptist	URC	Inde-pendent	Afro-Carib-bean	Pente-costal	Other	TOTAL Free Churches	Anglican	Roman Catholic	TOTAL Christian[1]
	1	*0*	*0*	*3*	*0*	*0*	*0*	*4*	*95*	*1*	*100*
Children attending:											
1985	200	0	0	1,700	100	0	0	2,000	37,400	1,100	40,500
⇩ 4 years	−50%	–	–	+94%	0%	–	–	+75%	−10%	+18%	−4%
1989	100	0	0	3,300	100	0	0	3,500	33,800	1,300	38,700
Percentage of total ⇨ %	*0*	*0*	*0*	*9*	*0*	*0*	*0*	*9*	*88*	*3*	*100*
Adults attending:											
1985	500	100	0	14,900	100	0	★	15,600	149,500	4,400	169,600
⇩ 4 years	0%	0%	–	+17%	0%	–	–	+16%	−7%	−11%	−5%
1989	500	100	0	17,400	100	0	★	18,100	139,400	3,900	161,500
Percentage of total ⇨ %	*0*	*0*	–	*11*	*0*	–	–	*11*	*86*	*3*	*100*
Membership:											
1985	400	100	0	12,200	★	0	0	12,700	174,700	43,200	230,800
⇩ 4 years	0%	0%	–	−33%	–	–	–	−31%	−9%	+18%	−5%
1989	400	100	0	8,200	100	0	0	8,800	159,400	50,900	219,400
Percentage of total ⇨ %	*0*	*0*	–	*4*	*0*	–	–	*4*	*73*	*23*	*100*
Percentage ⇩ of churches in each category (vertical total 100%) whose **adult attendance** 1985-1989:											
Grew %	†	–	–	(25)	–	–	–	(40)	25	(33)	25
Remained static %	†	–	–	(75)	–	–	–	(60)	68	(34)	68
Declined %	†	–	–	(0)	–	–	–	(0)	7	(33)	7

[1] This column includes Orthodox Church figures for child attendance of 100 and 100; adult attendance of 100 and 100; and membership of 200 and 300 for 1985 and 1989 respectively with 3 congregations in 1989

Year church/congregation founded

	Before 1500	1500-1799	1800-1849	1850-1874	1875-1899	1900-1924	1925-1949	1950-1974	1975 or later	ALL Churches
Percentage of all churches 1989 ⇨ %	*41*	*4*	*9*	*14*	*13*	*8*	*5*	*6*	*0*	*100*
Percentage ⇩ of churches in each category (vertical total 100%) whose **adult attendance** 1985-1989:										
Grew %	28	25	25	29	11	23	24	27	–	25
Remained static %	65	59	69	66	78	75	68	67	–	68
Declined %	7	16	6	5	11	2	8	6	–	7

Types of Third World Community Aid church would support

	Project activities	Specific Geographical area	Named communities	Named individuals	Administered through local churches	Evangelism/ missionary work	Other	No support	TOTAL ALL Churches
Percentage of all churches 1989 ⇨ %	*41*	*24*	*16*	*17*	*39*	*40*	*2*	*2*	*181[1]*
Percentage ⇩ of churches in each category (vertical total 100%) whose **adult attendance** 1985-1989:									
Grew %	24	30	23	31	25	20	37	0	25
Remained static %	70	60	65	61	68	72	63	82	68
Declined %	6	10	12	8	7	8	0	18	7

[1] Figures sum to more than *100%* because multiple answers were possible

Age and sex of churchgoers 1989

Age-Group	Churchgoers in 1989			Population 1989		
	Men %	Women %	Total %	Men %	Women %	Total %
Under 15	8	11	19	10	9	19
15-19	5	4	9	4	4	8
20-29	3	5	8	8	8	16
30-44	7	10	17	10	10	20
45-64	10	14	24	11	11	22
65 and over	7	16	23	6	9	15
All ages	40	60	100	49	51	100

Church environment

Percentage of all churches 1989 %	City Centre 3	Inner City 10	Council Estate 7	Suburban/ Urban Fringe 22	Separate Town 9	Other built-up area 4	Rural area: Commuter dormitory 18	Rural area: Other 27	ALL Churches 100
Children attending:									
1985	900	3,300	3,200	13,600	4,400	1,800	7,800	5,500	40,500
⇩ 4 years	+11%	0%	−3%	−2%	+2%	−6%	−9%	−15%	−4%
1989	1,000	3,300	3,100	13,300	4,500	1,700	7,100	4,700	38,700
Percentage of total ⇨ %	3	9	8	34	12	4	18	12	100
Adults attending:									
1985	7,600	16,200	11,200	57,600	21,300	8,300	26,000	21,400	169,600
⇩ 4 years	−7%	−7%	−5%	−6%	+1%	−6%	−5%	−4%	−5%
1989	7,100	15,100	10,600	54,200	21,500	7,800	24,700	20,500	161,500
Percentage of total ⇨ %	4	9	7	34	13	5	15	13	100
Membership:									
1985	8,000	22,700	19,100	80,000	29,900	11,000	33,000	27,100	230,800
⇩ 4 years	−1%	−6%	−21%	−4%	0%	+1%	−4%	−7%	−5%
1989	7,900	21,400	15,000	77,000	30,000	11,100	31,700	25,300	219,400
Percentage of total ⇨ %	4	10	7	35	14	5	14	11	100
Percentage of churches in each category (vertical total 100%) whose **adult attendance** 1985-1989:									
Grew %	(22)	11	25	24	22	(35)	31	31	25
Remained static %	(78)	83	68	68	63	(58)	65	64	68
Declined %	(0)	6	7	8	15	(7)	4	5	7
Percentage of churches in each category (vertical total 100%) in 1985 whose **services** were held:									
Morning only %	†	50	(24)	22	(44)	†	32	53	42
Morning & Evening %	†	50	(76)	76	(44)	†	64	32	49
Evening only %	†	0	(0)	2	(12)	†	4	15	9
Percentage of churches in each category (vertical total 100%) in 1989 whose **services** were held:									
Morning only %	(19)	(41)	28	32	54	(27)	55	49	43
Morning & Evening %	(68)	(54)	67	64	42	(68)	33	47	47
Evening only %	(13)	(5)	5	4	4	(5)	22	14	10

Size[1] of church by weekly adult attendance 1989

	10 or under	11-25	26-50	51- 100	101- 150	151- 200	201- 300	301- 400	401- 500	Over 500	Average size[1]	Number (=100%)
ALL Churches 1989 %	1	6	22	29	27	10	3	1	½	½	84	2,050
Growing churches %	0	4	14	21	32	20	7	1	½	½	108	513
Static churches %	1	7	24	30	27	7	2	1	½	½	77	1,393
Declining churches %	3	8	20	47	14	8	—	—	—	—	61	144

[1] Total of morning and evening services (where both held) with those attending both times counted twice

CATHOLIC[1]

1989 Catholic[1] adult church attendance as percentage of adult population: 3.7%

1989 Catholic[1] adult church attendance as percentage of all adult church attendance: 39%

1989 Catholic[1] child church attendance as percentage of child population: 5.1%

1989 Catholic[1] child church attendance as percentage of all child church attendance: 37%

Denomination of church and people

Percentage of all churches 1989 %	Metho-dist	Baptist	URC	Inde-pendent	Afro-Carib-bean	Pente-costal	Other	TOTAL Free Churches	Anglican	Roman Catholic	TOTAL Christian[2]
	1	0	0	2	0	0	0	3	44	53	100
Children attending:											
1985	500	100	200	1,000	100	300	★	2,200	48,100	419,800	470,100
⇩ 4 years	0%	0%	0%	+40%	0%	−33%	−	+18%	−12%	−3%	−4%
1989	500	100	200	1,400	100	200	100	2,600	42,500	405,700	450,900
Percentage of total ⇨ %	½							½	9½	90	100
Adults attending:											
1985	4,000	400	700	10,000	6,300	700	200	22,300	140,900	1,303,100	1,466,300
⇩ 4 years	+35%	+25%	+71%	+47%	−8%	−71%	+50%	+26%	+2%	−2%	−2%
1989	5,400	500	1,200	14,700	5,800	200	300	28,100	143,800	1,272,200	1,444,200
Percentage of total ⇨ %	½		1	½				2	10	88	100
Membership:											
1985	4,000	1,700	2,000	11,000	9,600	100	300	28,700	162,500	3,861,200	4,054,300
⇩ 4 years	+18%	+18%	0%	+5%	−19%	0%	0%	−1%	−16%	+4%	+3%
1989	4,700	2,000	2,000	11,600	7,800	100	300	28,500	136,900	4,026,200	4,193,300
Percentage of total ⇨ %	1							1	3	96	100
Percentage ⇩ of churches in each category (vertical total 100%) whose **adult attendance** 1985-1989:											
Grew %	35	−	−	22	−	−	−	35	26	16	21
Remained static %	58	−	−	75	−	−	−	59	70	72	71
Declined %	7	−	−	3	−	−	−	6	4	12	8

[2] This column includes Orthodox Church figures for child attendance of 0 and 100; adult attendance of ★ and 100; and membership of 1,900 and 1,700 for 1985 and 1989 respectively with 3 congregations in 1989

Year church/congregation founded

	Before 1500	1500-1799	1800-1849	1850-1874	1875-1899	1900-1924	1925-1949	1950-1974	1975 or later	ALL Churches
Percentage of all churches 1989 ⇨ %	25	4	9	10	12	9	12	16	3	100
Percentage ⇩ of churches in each category (vertical total 100%) whose **adult attendance** 1985-1989:										
Grew %	29	14	28	21	20	21	16	19	12	23
Remained static %	70	83	70	75	75	75	79	75	84	74
Declined %	1	3	2	4	5	4	5	6	4	3

Types of Third World Community Aid church would support

Percentage of all churches 1989 ⇨ %	Project activities	Specific Geographical area	Named communities	Named individuals	Administered through local churches	Evangelism/ missionary work	Other	No support	TOTAL ALL Churches
	56	21	19	15	36	37	1	1	186[3]
Percentage ⇩ of churches in each category (vertical total 100%) whose **adult attendance** 1985-1989:									
Grew %	19	21	18	19	21	26	20	12	21
Remained static %	73	70	76	73	73	60	77	81	71
Declined %	8	9	6	8	6	10	3	7	8

[1] This term is used here in a churchmanship, not denominational, sense and includes non-Roman Catholics
[3] Figures sum to more than *100%* because multiple answers were possible

Age and sex of churchgoers 1989

Age-Group	Churchgoers in 1989			Population 1989		
	Men %	Women %	Total %	Men %	Women %	Total %
Under 15	11	13	24	10	9	19
15-19	4	5	9	4	4	8
20-29	5	5	10	8	8	16
30-44	7	10	17	10	10	20
45-64	10	13	23	11	11	22
65 and over	7	10	17	6	9	15
All ages	44	56	100	49	51	100

Church environment

Percentage of all churches 1989 %	City Centre 2	Inner City 7	Council Estate 9	Suburban/ Urban Fringe 24	Separate Town 14	Other built-up area 4	Rural area: Commuter dormitory 16	Rural area: Other 24	ALL Churches 100
Children attending:									
1985	22,600	52,500	43,600	166,400	68,700	19,100	53,000	44,200	470,100
⇩ 4 years	−14%	−5%	+5%	−5%	−4%	+1%	−1%	−10%	−4%
1989	19,400	50,100	45,800	158,500	65,900	19,300	52,300	39,600	450,900
Percentage of total ⇨ %	4	11	10	35	15	4	12	9	100
Adults attending:									
1985	83,100	202,700	197,900	491,000	218,400	61,800	106,400	105,000	1,466,300
⇩ 4 years	−2%	−6%	−8%	0%	+1%	+2%	+4%	−3%	−2%
1989	81,400	191,400	181,700	493,300	220,600	63,000	111,100	101,700	1,444,200
Percentage of total ⇨ %	6	13	13	34	15	4	8	7	100
Membership:									
1985	257,600	536,700	528,500	1,468,500	625,000	143,600	280,400	214,000	4,054,300
⇩ 4 years	−2%	−1%	+2%	+4%	+7%	+7%	+6%	+4%	+3%
1989	251,700	532,800	539,500	1,528,700	666,900	153,800	296,300	223,600	4,193,300
Percentage of total ⇨ %	6	13	13	36	16	4	7	5	100
Percentage of churches in each category (vertical total 100%) whose **adult attendance** 1985-1989:									
Grew %	(11)	17	19	20	19	(26)	27	21	21
Remained static %	(78)	69	71	70	75	(72)	65	75	71
Declined %	(11)	14	10	10	6	(2)	8	4	8
Percentage of churches in each category (vertical total 100%) in 1985 whose **services** were held:									
Morning only %	(0)	20	23	18	7	23	17	25	15
Morning & Evening %	(90)	70	66	72	83	67	72	63	74
Evening only %	(10)	10	11	10	10	10	11	12	11
Percentage of churches in each category (vertical total 100%) in 1989 whose **services** were held:									
Morning only %	(0)	25	35	11	11	19	13	23	17
Morning & Evening %	(90)	63	54	79	78	71	75	63	71
Evening only %	(10)	12	11	10	11	10	12	14	12

Size[1] of church by weekly adult attendance 1989

	10 or under	11-25	26-50	51-100	101-150	151-200	201-300	301-400	401-500	Over 500	Average size[1]	Number (=100%)
ALL Churches 1989 %	1	2	4	14	16	16	11	10	10	16	242	6,205
Growing churches %	0	1	0	16	12	15	14	12	11	19	287	1,309
Static churches %	2	1	6	14	18	16	10	9	9	15	230	4,429
Declining churches %	0	6	7	11	19	19	13	12	5	8	195	467

[1] Total of morning and evening services (where both held) with those attending both times counted twice

ALL OTHER CHURCHMANSHIPS

1989 All Other Churchmanships adult church attendance as percentage of adult population: **0.1%**

1989 All Other Churchmanships adult church attendance as percentage of all adult church attendance: **2%**

1989 All Other Churchmanships child church attendance as percentage of child population: **0.2%**

1989 All Other Churchmanships child church attendance as percentage of all child church attendance: **1%**

Denomination of church and people

Percentage of all churches	Metho-dist	Baptist	URC	Inde-pendent	Afro-Carib-bean	Pente-costal	Other	TOTAL Free Churches	Anglican	Roman Catholic	TOTAL Christian[1]
1989 ⇨ %	25	4	6	8	1	3	7	54	36	1	100
Children attending:											
1985	2,700	300	700	1,400	800	400	200	6,500	2,900	1,200	13,300
⇩ 4 years	−15%	0%	−14%	+43%	−13%	+25%	+50%	+3%	−7%	+17%	+2%
1989	2,300	300	600	2,000	700	500	300	6,700	2,700	1,400	13,500
Percentage of total ⇨ %	17	2	5	15	5	4	2	50	20	10	100[2]
Adults attending:											
1985	9,000	1,000	2,200	3,000	1,300	1,300	1,300	19,100	20,300	11,500	58,900
⇩ 4 years	−1%	0%	+9%	+73%	+8%	+92%	+23%	+20%	−14%	−2%	+3%
1989	8,900	1,000	2,400	5,200	1,400	2,500	1,600	23,000	17,400	11,300	60,500
Percentage of total ⇨ %	15	2	4	8	2	4	3	38	29	19	100[3]
Membership:											
1985	10,000	1,000	2,400	4,000	1,000	1,500	2,600	22,500	31,200	29,200	297,600
⇩ 4 years	−2%	−10%	0%	+40%	+30%	+80%	+15%	+14%	−42%	+14%	+2%
1989	9,800	900	2,400	5,600	1,300	2,700	3,000	25,700	18,200	33,200	303,700
Percentage of total ⇨ %	3	0	1	2	0	1	1	8	6	11	100[4]
Percentage ⇩ of churches in each category (vertical total 100%) whose **adult attendance** 1985-1989:											
Grew %	10	(20)	(25)	(25)	(40)	(63)	(0)	22	13	(51)	18
Remained static %	75	(80)	(75)	(75)	(40)	(24)	(80)	67	80	(49)	73
Declined %	15	(0)	(0)	(0)	(20)	(13)	(20)	11	7	(0)	9

[1] This column includes Orthodox Church figures for child attendance of 2,700 and 2,700; adult attendance of 8,000 and 8,800; and membership of 214,700 and 226,600 for 1985 and 1989 respectively with 90 congregations in 1989 (= 9% of total All Others)
[2] Including 20% for Orthodox Churches [3] Including 14% for Orthodox Churches [4] Including 75% for Orthodox Churches

Year church/congregation founded

	Before 1500	1500-1799	1800-1849	1850-1874	1875-1899	1900-1924	1925-1949	1950-1974	1975 or later	ALL Churches
Percentage of all churches **1989** ⇨ %	25	9	14	8	12	7	4	12	9	100
Percentage ⇩ of churches in each category (vertical total 100%) whose **adult attendance** 1985-1989:										
Grew %	9	20	18	8	4	9	11	35	69	18
Remained static %	85	73	72	92	86	63	78	54	20	73
Declined %	6	7	10	0	10	28	11	11	11	9

Types of Third World Community Aid church would support

Percentage of all churches **1989** ⇨ %	Project activities	Specific Geographical area	Named communities	Named individuals	Administered through local churches	Evangelism/missionary work	Other	No support	TOTAL ALL Churches
	37	17	11	12	37	40	4	7	165[1]
Percentage ⇩ of churches in each category (vertical total 100%) whose **adult attendance** 1985-1989:									
Grew %	13	39	16	15	14	19	9	48	18
Remained static %	80	47	73	74	73	77	91	18	73
Declined %	7	14	11	11	13	4	0	34	9

[1] Figures sum to more than 100% because multiple answers were possible

ALL OTHER CHURCHMANSHIPS

Age and sex of churchgoers 1989

Age-Group	Churchgoers in 1989			Population 1989		
	Men %	Women %	Total %	Men %	Women %	Total %
Under 15	8	10	18	10	9	19
15-19	3	3	6	4	4	8
20-29	5	6	11	8	8	16
30-44	7	10	17	10	10	20
45-64	9	14	23	11	11	22
65 and over	9	16	25	6	9	15
All ages	41	59	100	49	51	100

Church environment

Percentage of all churches 1989 %	City Centre 1	Inner City 8	Council Estate 5	Suburban/ Urban Fringe 17	Separate Town 8	Other built-up area 3	Rural area: Commuter dormitory 19	Rural area: Other 39	ALL Churches 100
Children attending:									
1985	200	1,600	1,300	4,100	1,100	500	1,700	2,800	13,300
⇩ 4 years	+50%	+81%	−38%	−5%	+18%	−40%	0%	−18%	+2%
1989	300	2,900	800	3,900	1,300	300	1,700	2,300	13,500
Percentage of total ⇨ %	2	21	6	29	10	2	13	17	100
Adults attending:									
1985	1,500	11,700	2,800	17,200	6,600	1,200	6,100	11,800	58,900
⇩ 4 years	−7%	+1%	+4%	+3%	+8%	0%	+5%	+2%	+3%
1989	1,400	11,800	2,900	17,700	7,100	1,200	6,400	12,000	60,500
Percentage of total ⇨ %	2	20	5	27	12	2	10	20	100
Membership:									
1985	4,100	133,700	9,100	73,800	14,700	3,500	24,700	34,000	297,600
⇩ 4 years	−5%	0%	−3%	+13%	+15%	0%	−3%	−10%	+2%
1989	3,900	133,100	8,800	83,100	16,900	3,500	23,900	30,500	303,700
Percentage of total ⇨ %	1	44	3	27	6	1	8	10	100
Percentage of churches in each category (vertical total 100%) whose **adult attendance** 1985-1989:									
Grew %	†	(38)	(16)	(23)	(15)	†	(18)	14	18
Remained static %	†	(54)	(76)	(65)	(77)	†	(73)	77	73
Declined %	†	(8)	(8)	(12)	(8)	†	(9)	9	9
Percentage of churches in each category (vertical total 100%) in 1985 whose **services** were held:									
Morning only %	†	(6)	(63)	26	(8)	†	19	15	18
Morning & Evening %	†	(94)	(25)	74	(92)	†	79	72	74
Evening only %	†	(0)	(12)	0	(0)	†	2	13	8
Percentage of churches in each category (vertical total 100%) in 1989 whose **services** were held:									
Morning only %	†	(7)	(70)	32	(10)	†	23	17	22
Morning & Evening %	†	(92)	(20)	68	(90)	†	75	68	71
Evening only %	†	(1)	(10)	0	(0)	†	2	15	7

Size[1] of church by weekly adult attendance 1989

		10 or under	11-25	26-50	51- 100	101- 150	151- 200	201- 300	301- 400	401- 500	Over 500	Average size[1]	Number (=100%)
ALL Churches 1989	%	3	18	31	21	14	6	4	1	1	1	70	956
Growing churches	%	0	10	18	24	22	18	6	0	1	1	97	172
Static churches	%	2	19	34	20	14	3	5	1	1	1	68	698
Declining churches	%	21	29	22	21	0	7	—	—	—	—	33	86

[1] Total of morning and evening services (where both held) with those attending both times counted twice

ACKNOWLEDGEMENTS

A small army of people have helped in various ways with the English Church Census. The key players have been mentioned in the dedication and a huge debt is owed to them all.

Behind the original Board members stood those who came later and supported the decision that had already been taken: Viscountess Brentford, Brian Quick, Dr Harri Heino, Bryant Myers. Within MARC Europe the project owes much to the helpfulness of Mary Lawson, Research Department Secretary, who kept numerous ends tied together. Others in the department helped at various stages including Research Assistants Angela Johnson and Cate Partridge, but a special load fell on Jon Blake, Senior Research Manager, in the early part of 1990 when the computerisation programme was at its height. Later members of the Research Department, Boyd Myers and Lindsey Marshall, have helped with the interpretation and the writing of Regional commentaries. Our former Director of Research, Phil Back, also kindly helped with these, as did Stephen Brierley and Greg Smith.

Enormous thanks are due too to John Marcus who computerised some 16 pages of equations to ensure that the estimates were as reasonable as possible, and who coped at short notice with numerous requests for extra printouts. Many people helped put data into the computer in the first place and we are grateful to Arthur Richards for helping to organise our computer to allow this to happen easily. Val Hiscock was one who did much herself and helped to organise others such as Patricia Dyer, Doreen Dewar and Yvonne Parfett, and those who worked with them — Gboyinwa Ajayi, Rose Atfield, Pam Bell, Linda Bloomfield, Philip Elledge, Jeremy Longley, Angela Major, Dorothy Mayhew, Celia Thomas and Carol Upton (née Davies).

But before the results could be computerised, they had to be collected, and that collection meant sending out 38,000 forms and two reminders. It was not a simple process. Many ministers look after more than one church, and so the forms were grouped together in suitable multiples of two, three, four, even up to ten or more. Many helped get the forms ready for posting under the supervision of Betty Reed including Funola Craig, Julie Evans, Margaret Evans, Ruth Evans, Gene Fellows, Peggy Hale, Laurence Hobbs, Allen Milner, Joan Milner, Tim Murdoch, Steve Rawcliffe, Harriet Rowbottom, Jonathan Southby and Keith York.

The forms had to be sent out, and some people were exceptionally helpful in aiding the identification of all the individual churches. Commissioner Harry Read of the Salvation Army and Pastor John Arthur of the Seventh-Day Adventist Church made sure we had complete lists. Douglas Fryer at Church House graciously guided us in the labyrinth of Anglican Churches and helped us secure extra data at short notice. Bryan Tolhurst at the Methodist Conference Office and Carole Rogers of the United Reformed Church gave good help too. The excellent responses from these churches reflected their co-operation for which we are most grateful.

Many others also helped us get as complete a list as possible. Graham Fisher for the Gospel Standard Baptist Churches, Chester Woodhall of the Churches of Christ, Rev Milum Kostic of the Serbian Orthodox Church, Dr John Boyes for the Christian Brethren (Open), Mike Stockdale for Bristol Churches, Joel Edwards of the Afro-Caribbean Evangelical Alliance, Evan M Lisbund of the Pentecostal Help Organisation, Rev Rocky Scott of Redemption Church for black-led churches, and Molly Porter ex-Administrator of the Zebra Project. Robert Beckford helped with the Wesleyan Holiness Churches, Pastor Abraham Oshuntola of the Pentecostal Gospel Faith Chapel, and Mike Clarke with the Bibleway Group. We also received advice from the Evangelical Alliance, Evangelical Missionary Alliance, World Vision of Britain, Hampstead Bible School, Church Army and the major House Church groups — Harvestime, Pioneer, New Frontiers, Ichthus Fellowship — and Tankerton Evangelical Church, the Coign Fellowship, Zion Baptist Church at Creech St Michael and many, many others who telephoned or wrote.

I am grateful for the excellent work by Dee Frankling and Lois Pratt on the regular staff of MARC Europe who helped in typing the commentary on the results, 'Christian' England, and to Betty Reed and Rachael Wickington who helped when Suzanne Wardall broke her arm at the critical time. Books and tables had to be proofread, and Lesley Reynolds and Allen Milner did a very good job on this as well.

Alec Hitchins put in hours upon hours of both creative thinking and detailed art direction into the illustrations. Roland Pearson helped with all the diagrams in this book, managing to cope despite the tedium of doing so many similar items one after the other.

Philippa King, David Longley and Chris Radley all had major inputs in the critical area of publicity for the venture.

Without the contributions of 27,000 who kindly completed the forms, however, all would have been in vain, and to these thousands who thus helped make the Census a success many, many grateful thanks. It was clear that a good number went to much trouble to give accurate figures.

Special thanks are due to the great patience of the printer, David Hunt, who not only sorted out all the mass of paper, but took a personal interest to ensure it was as accurate as it could be. Likewise thanks are due to his incredible typesetter who has set in this volume approximately 250,000 numbers at an error rate of less than 1 in 1,000. Such attention to detail is the hallmark of quality and for this precision we are most grateful.

All the responsibility for the final version of the text is mine, but the editing of it at very short notice and in a short time span was willingly undertaken by Jenny Rogers, whose willingness to contribute and help in the expert way in which only she can, encouraged me enormously. Likewise we are grateful to those on the Council of Reference who kindly gave advice and supported the project in key ways, gallantly reading the draft of this book in a short period of time. We especially respect the hours taken by Eileen Barker, Richard Bewes, Sir John Boreham, Bernard Green, David Jackman, Stuart Murray, Alan Rogers, Peter Searle, Michael Hornsby-Smith, Basil Varnam, and David Winter and to several of these and to Roger Forster, Malcolm Laver, Michael Lawson and Keith Roberts for subsequent discussions. Thanks are due too to Valerie Passmore for copy-editing the book, also at short notice.

The printed book may bear my name but it is clear from this list of people that this is above all a team project. A body has many parts and each part is important for the fulfilment of the work of that body. In the English Church Census many people have played a role and each has contributed to a vital element in the whole. Long hours worked, evening after evening, enthusiasm shown, and the sheer willingness to help in any way that was necessary, made this an exercise which we all sincerely hope will help the Church in this country move forward, and which has also challenged and inspired us to give, and having done all, still to give, for the good of the Kingdom.

Peter Brierley
February 1991